Śrī Vijaya Bhairavar

(A Terrifying, Sacred, Divine form of Lord Shiva)

*

Dr. Ramamurthy N.

M.Sc., B.G.L., CA‖ B, CCP, DSADP, CISA, PMP, CGBL, Ph.D.

*

Title: *Śrī Vijaya Bhairavar*
                         (A Terrifying, Sacred, Divine form of Lord Shiva)

First Edition: 2021

Author: **Dr. Ramamurthy N**, Chennai.
                      http://ramamurthy.jāgruti.co.in/

Copyright ©:   With the author (No part of this book may be reproduced in any manner whatsoever without the written permission from the author).

Number of pages: 152

Price: ₹ 200.00

ISBN (13):   978-93-82237-87-7

Printed at:

Published by:

Table of Contents

Date : 04/09/2021

Introduction

ॐ गुरुर्ब्रह्मा गुरुर्विष्णु: गुरुर्देवो महेश्वर: |
गुरुसाक्षात् परंब्रह्म तस्मै श्री गुरवे नम: ॥

ॐ गजाननं भूतगणादि सेव्हितं कपित्थजम्बूफलसार भक्षितम् |
उमासुतं शोकविनाशकारणं नमामि विघ्नेश्वर पादपङ्कजम् ॥

All of us might have heard of *Sri Bhairava Devar*. However, most of us might not know in detail about him. Salem Sri Vidya Ashramam, a holy place for worship, has a beautiful idol of *Sri Vidhya Swarna Vijaya Bhairavar*. This book is intended to clarify about this Devar for those who come to worship here and want to know in detail about him. It is apt that the same Salem Sri Vidya Ashramam[1] has also published this book.

There are three forms of Lord Shiva – *Bogam*, *Yogam* and *Vegam*. The speed (*Vegam*) form is called Bhairavar. Worshiping him will solve all the difficulties of deeds, greed, the enemy of debt, etc.

Beginning with the introduction, this is book is structured as;

* *Śrī Vijaya Bhairavar*
* Form of *Bhairava Devar*
* *Śrī Bhairava Mantras*
* *Śrī Bhairava Yantram* – an introduction
* *Śrī Bhairava* Pooja
* *Śrī Bhairava Deva Homa* – an overview
* *Śrī Aṣṭabhairava Dhyāna Stotram*
* *Śrī Bhairava Sarva Phalaprada Stotram*
* *Śrī Bhairava Aṣṭakam*
* *Śrī Bhairava Aṣṭotra Śata Nāmāvaliḥ*
* *Śrī Bhairava Sahasranāma Stotram*
* *Śrī Bhairava Kavacam*

---

[1] More details about this Ashramam have been provided in a separate chapter.

In Samskrutam, *Kavacam* means armour. The above *Śrī Bhairava Kavacam* is very powerful. This is part of *Śrī Viśvanātha Tantra* text. This is called as *Mantragarbham* i.e., pregnant with *mantras*. One who recites this powerful armour of *Bhairava Devar*, becomes victorious everywhere and gets every kind of material comfort. He becomes fearless and gets respected everywhere. This *Kavaca* removes the negative energies from within and from outside.

Primarily, the aim of this book is to explain in detail, the incarnation of Lord Shiva as Bhairava, to explain his form and purpose and to explain some of the mantras. It is believed that the devotees will get benefitted by reading and understanding this and worshiping Sri Bhairavar in the right and appropriate way.

Devotees are advised to consult a qualified scholar or guru, if they have any doubts about any mantras or worshipping methods mentioned in this book. It is highly suggested not to start recitation/ puja with half-knowledge and assuming the rest. Books can only be a reference guide, but cannot act as a teacher (guru).

Conventions used in this book: The transliterated Samskruta words are written in italics — for instance *Dharma*. When Samskruta words are transliterated in English diacritical marks are used to correctly pronounce the words. Wherever possible the hymns are provided both in English and Samskrutam.

This book is simultaneously written in Tamil also.

My humble *pranāms* to *Śrīśrī Praṇavānunda Saraswati Swāmijī* of Ayyarmalai, at whose instance this book has been written. Also, he has given his blessings and some pleasantries about this edition.

My sincere thanks are due to all those who supported in this noble cause of bring out this book. Hope the readers would be benefitted by the contents of this book. The readers are requested to feel free to send their feedback and comments.

Our humble *Praṇāms* to all our *Gurus*.

Om Tat Sat

Chennai
2021   *Dr. Ramamurthy N*

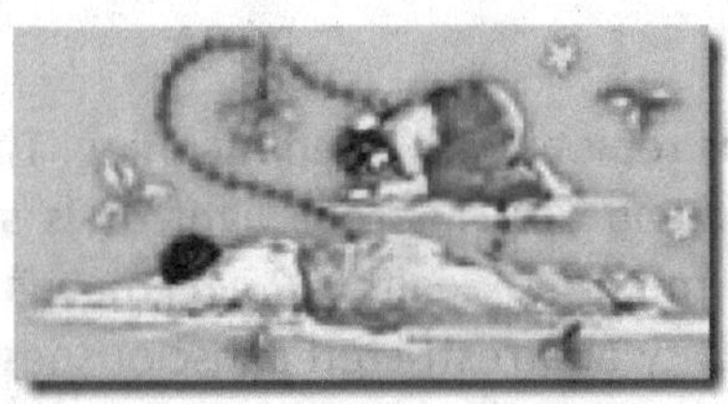

*****

Lord Bhairavar

Om Śrī Bhairvāya Namaḥ

Lord *Bhairavar*, usually called as *Kāla Bhairavar* is a fierce manifestation of Lord Shiva and is highly revered across the Indian sub-continent.

The name *Bhairava* itself is replete with deep meaning. The first syllable '*Bhai*' means fear and also lustrous light. It is said to endow the devotee with material wealth. '*Rava*' means echo. While '*Ra*' casts off negativity and restricted consciousness, '*Va*' keeps creating opportunities. In totality *Bhairava* denotes that by using fear we can attain '*aseem anand*' or extreme endless delight. Worshipped by Hindus, Jains and Buddhists alike, daily prayer offerings to Bhairava helps in achieving success, defeating enemies and attaining all materialistic comforts. He helps devotees fruitfully utilize their time in securing their goals. This is the reason why he is known as the Lord of Time (*kāla*). Wasting time in trivial pursuits can be diverted towards a constructive purpose, if one offers prayers and chants the name of *Bhairava*. He purifies souls with his sheer power and makes odds favorable for believers. Almost miraculously, one is at the right place at the right time for the best of opportunities.

Tibetan Buddhist texts mention about 84 types of Bhairava forms and meditative practices for each of them. The Vajrayana text refers to Vajra Bhairava and his consort Vajravarahi.

The Jain religion speaks in great detail about the worship of Bhairava. 96 Bhairava forms are described. The most elaborate Upasana norms can be used to express the aspirations of the world. The Sekkhizhar, Tamil poet, says that the Jains refer to this achievement of overcoming the aspirations as "the benefit of our religious worship".

During the time when Sri Adi Shankara lived in Varanasi, while bathing in the Ganges, the Lord took this form only and came in front of him, to bless him the 'Brahmajanam' (knowledge of brahmam)[2].

The word Bhairava itself has considerable prominence in invocations. Chanting the three syllables *'bhai'*, *'ra'* and *'va'* is said to create a bounty of benefits. The sacred sound is said to be a reminder that each second is precious and that one should not procrastinate and disrespect time. Instead, one must polish oneself by chanting and sharpen ones focus by chanting.

According to many gurus, devotees must chant these syllables 108 times a day, anytime day or night. One can even chant the mantra more than 108 times or by writing 1,008 or 10,008 times for great outcomes and protection.

Lord Bhairava is also known as *'Kotwal'* or *'Kshetpālaka'*, the guardian of the city. The keys to *Shiva* and *Shakti* temples are ceremonially submitted to *Bhairava* at the closing time and received from him at the opening time in the morning. There is generally a shrine dedicated to him in the North-east corner of all the Shiva temple premises. He is also a guardian of the travelers and blesses those who visit on pilgrimage. The *Siddhas* state that before embarking on a journey, especially while travelling at night, one must light lamps and garland Lord *Bhairava* with cashew nut garlands. This assures protection and safety. For those abroad away from the blessed shores, the worship is equally important.

There are many interesting legends surrounding Kala Bhairava, one of the eight avatars of Lord Shiva. The origin of the mighty god is attributed to a tale in the Shiv Mahapurana. Once Lord Brahma grew arrogant and egoistic. During those times he had five heads one on top of the four heads. He commanded Lord Vishnu to worship him, as he is the creator of the universe. Lord Shiva wanted to teach him a lesson and make him more committed and responsible to his task. Therefore, he created *Kāla Bhairava* from his nail and thus *Kāla Bhairava* manifested as an incarnation of

---

[2] In most of the texts this form is mentioned as Chandala

Lord Shiva to punish Lord Brahma. *Kāla Bhairava* beheaded one of Brahma's five heads.

According to Sookshmagamam, Kriyapatham, there is a different story. Once, Brahma saw his daughter Tilottamai and became obsessed with lust and ran after her. Not to accept this unjust act, she ran taking a form of a deer. Brahma also took the form of a deer and followed. When Brahma tried to do so, Lord Shiva came as a hunter and cut off one of the Brahma's heads with a sharp arrow. Due to that Lord Shiva got the name Ajari.

Since then, Brahma has four heads while Bhairava carries the fifth in one of his hands. But chopping off Brahma's head amounted to the killing of a Brahmin. Consequently, Bhairava had to carry the gruesome head with him for 12 years. He wandered like a vagabond, till he was liberated of the sin. Usually, the idol of Bhairava depicts him in this frightful form.

Despite being one of the most feared deities, he is essentially one of the most rewarding and protective Gods. In tantric practices he is called in a sacred way as *Batuka (Vatuka) Bhairava*. Being a *Rudra*, the Lord is said to be very knowledgeable in *tantra mantras*.

Kala Bhairava is also famous for his dog vehicle. The dog is usually seated on one side, ready to taste the dripping blood from the executed head of Brahma. Looking after and feeding dogs is thus considered to be another way of displaying devotion. *Bhairava* can bestow incredible blessings and the boon of auspicious time to devotees feeding to dogs. According to myths, if one feeds hungry dogs with "*halwa puri*" (sweet bread), then automatically all problems can be overcome.

People have always been worshipping *Kala Bhairava* from the days of yore. But according to the sacred texts the 60 years from last Chirtabhanu Year i.e., April 2002 to the next Chirtabhanu Year i.e., April 2062, is the most important time. The *Krishna Paksha Ashtami* (the eighth day after full moon) is said to be the most ideal day for puja rituals. Practitioners celebrate Kala

Bhairavashtami or Kala Bhairava Jayanti commemorating the day Kala Bhairava appeared on earth in the Margashirsha (Margazhi) month (December-January) of the Hindu calendar. There are elaborate ceremonies in the 12 Jyotirlinga Shiva shrines in Varanasi, Rameswaram, Ujjain and others, which have special rites and sacraments on this day.

Kala Bhairava has 8 manifestations, called as (*Ashtanga*) *Bhairavas* to protect this universe by creating lights from all the eight directions. They are –

1.   *Asithānga Bhairava,*
2.   *Ruru Bhairava,*
3.   *Chaṇḍa Bhairava,*
4.   *Krodha Bhairava,*
5.   *Unmattha Bhairava,*
6.   *Kapāla Bhairava,*
7.   *Bheeshana Bhairava* and
8.   *Samhāra Bhairava.*

In addition to these eight Bhairavas, *Aadhi Shaivaits* worshiped 64[3] types of *Bhairavas* also. It has been told that the Ashtanga Bhairavas, each with eight forms, 8 x 8 = 64 become 64 Bhairavas. There are idols of 64 *Bhairavas* in 64 stages on the banks of the Ganges in Varanasi.

Shakti Peetas are the sacred spots where the divine energy of the Mother Form is installed. It is believed that *Kāla Bhairava* guards all the 52 *Shaktipeetas*[4] and hence there are said to be 52 forms of *Bhairava* across the sacred spots. Since he guards the *shatipeetas* he is also known as '*Kotwal*'. Therefore, *Kāla Bhairava* is also called *Batuka Bhairav.* *Batuka Bhairav* is the most worshipped form of Bhairava in *tantra*. Protecting *Shakti* is significant for everlasting peace amidst the scenarios of wrath, violence and animosity. Prayers to Lord *Kala Bhairava* as well as

---

[3] These 64 Bhairavas have been listed in a separate chapter.
[4] There are different schools about number of *shatipeetas*. Srimad Devi Bhagavatam says there are 108 *shatipeetas*.

Sarabeshwara[5] and *Amruta Mrutyunjaya* are necessary for this safeguarding.

Bhairava holds within Himself the entire universe by reducing all the shaktis to sameness with Himself and inasmuch as He completely devours within Himself the entire mass of ideation (which is responsible for sense of difference) – *Shiva Sutras* say.

From the Aghoris and Kapalika sect to Gorat Kashmiris, from Assamese tantric practitioners to the Gowdas of Karnataka, from worshippers in Kathmandu to those in Sri Lanka, across diverse communities *Kala Bhairava* is venerated. The Kasi (Benares) Bhairava is accorded much reverence. Hindu reformer Adi Shankara once wrote a beautiful hymn titled *"Kala Bhairava Ashtakam*[6]*"* with 8 verses, in honour of the Kashi Bhairava deity. In the rural milieu of Tamil Nadu, Maharashtra and others, he is believed to be the village protector. The villagers erect decorative statues of "*grama devata*" at the village entrance.

Bhairava means 'terrifying' and it is an adjective applied to Shiva in his fearful aspect. Yet in Kashmir Shaivism, the three letters of this name are taken in a different manner. '*Bha*' means '*bharana*' – maintenance, '*ra*' means '*ravana*' – withdrawal and '*va*' means '*vamana*' – creation of the universe.

Kāla Bhairava is one of the most preferred deity for the Tantrics. The Rudrayamala Tantra, describes the worship of *Vatuka Bhairava*, or *Bhairava* as a small boy and gives his *mantra* as –

ॐ ह्रीं बटुकाय आपदुद्धारणाय कुरूकुरू बटुकाय ह्रीं ।

Om Hrīm Batukāya Āpaduddhāraṇaya Kuru Kuru Batukāya Hrīm.

Although the ascription to *Rudrayamala* is commonly found in the colophons of tantric texts, these passages do not appear in the modern work now available.

---

[5] *Sarabeshwara* is also called as *Ākāsha Bhairava*
[6] Given in a separate chapter

Kala Bhairava also called the keeper of time i.e., the lord who controls the time and incidents that take place in the human's life. The divine *Kala Bhairava* stands for *Kala*— the time period and Bhairava, the keeper of time.

By worshipping Lord Bhairava, one will attain the sheer power to control the time and the incidents that take place in his life with the blessings of *Kala Bhairava*. He blesses the devotee with the divine power of predicting things that are to happen and to avoid mishaps by controlling time.

By worshiping Lord Bhairava one can get rid of all the obstacles and enemies from his life. Lord Bhairava is worshiped on Sundays the day of Rahu Kala (between 4:30 and 6:00 p.m.) by Coconut, Flowers, Sindoor, Mustard oil, black till etc. He can be worshiped on all days also for early success.

According to Bhairavagamam, Lord Shiva does the task of creation by taking the Ananda Bhairava form, the task of protection by taking the Kala Bhairava form and the task of oppression by taking the Kalagni Bhairava form.

Let us all meditate upon and worship *Bhairava* and get benefitted. Thus, this fearful manifestation of Lord Shiva is believed to be one of the most protective powers blessing for humanity.

*****

Śrī Vijaya Bhairavar

*Om Bhairavāya Vidhmahē Harihara Brahmātmakāya Dhīmahi
Taṇṇaḥ Svarṇākarṣaṇa Bhairavaḥ Pracōdayāt ||*

The lord of wealth is called the *Bhairvar* of the Golden Attraction. In this form there is an *Akshaya* vessel instead of the skull in the left hand. It is said that the skull has been kept as a utensil because he is the giver of gold. The hope is that wealth will increase at home when devotees pray to him. Another highlight is the display with two dogs as vehicles.

Sri Swarnakarshana Bhairavar is also called as *Sri Vijaya Bhairavar*. At Sri Vidya Ashram, Salem, Sri Vidya Swarna Vijaya Bhairava, is bestowing his blessings on the devotees in the form of an eye-catching stone called *Sri Vijaya Bhairavar*.

All kinds of Bhairavas are the forms of Lord Shiva only. However, Sri Swarnakarshana Bhairava is unique among them. He is an aspect of Tri-murtis, Brahma, Vishnu and Rudran. His Ambal (consort) is Sri Swarnakarshini Trishakti.

He has an yellow coloured body, with four arms and three eyes. He also wears yellow coloured clothing and ornaments. In his four arms he holds, golden vessel, damaru (Udukkai), a goad (angusam) and a pasam. He is three-eyed. He is always with the best dog vehicle. He sits on a throne of nine-gems, under the Kalpa Viruksha (tree). With the light of the rising sun, the Lord wears crescent and is blessing his devotees.

In some of the idols, he is depicted as six-armed carrying a scepter, damaru, pasam, a goad (angusam), munda-siram (skull), sword, etc. In some places he is described as carrying a lotus flower, nectar in a golden vessel, showing the hand-signs of Vara-abhaya, a conch and a wheel (chakra) in six hands.

He is the ocean of mercy bestowing gold on the devotees.

If the following 12 names of Swarnakarshana Bhairava are chant daily after chanting his root mantra, the reciter will get all the desired, especially more gold – says *mantra shastras*.

1. *Om Svarṇa Pradāya Namaḥ*
2. *Om Svarṇa Varṣiṇē Namaḥ*
3. *Om Svarṇākarṣaṇa Bhairavāya Namaḥ*
4. *Om Bhakta Priyāya Namaḥ*
5. *Om Bhakta Vaṣyāya Namaḥ*
6. *Om Bhaktābīṣṭa Phalapradāya Namaḥ*
7. *Om Siddhidāya Namaḥ*
8. *Om Karuṇā Mūrttayē Namaḥ*
9. *Om Praṇadābhīṣṭa Pūrṇatāya Namaḥ*
10. *Om Niti Siddhi Pradāya Namaḥ*
11. *Om Svarṇa Siddhi Pradāya Namaḥ*
12. *Om Rasa Siddhi Pradāya Namaḥ*

He will also give his devotees the ability to create gold (alchemy). And he will also make it easy for those who are in trouble to get out of it.

It is mentioned in some texts that he would sit in the business establishments. Having his *yantra* (wheel) or a picture or a statue in a place of business, such as a shop, seems to increase business and increase profits.

Through the mantra of "*Dhāridraya Vidveṣaṇāya*" it is very clear that poverty will never show its head to those who worship him. It is also known that the devotee will live for many years as a wealthy man.

The root *mantra* of *Swarnakarshana Bhairav* has to be chant daily, applying sandal paste to the Lord and offering honey for 1,000 times with concentration. The devotee will to get the 'treasure'. A win is sure in all his affairs. Thus, it is mentioned in the book "*Vijaya Saravali*".

Thus, the glorious Swarnakarshana Bhairav, with the name of Sri Vijaya Bhairav, alongwith his consort, as a couple, is giving darshan, at Salem Srividya Ashram. Pujas are performed daily on behalf of the devotees to bless them. Special recitation, Homam, etc. are held on special days.

Let us all bow and surrender to that Sri Vijaya Bhairav.

*****

Forms of *Bhairava Devar*

Om Kālakālāya Vidmahe Kālāthītāya Dhīmahi
Thanno Kālabhairava Prachodayāth ‖

Om Śvāna Vāhanāya Vidmahe Śūla Hasthāya Dhīmahi
Thanno Bhairava Prachodayāth ‖

Usually, the meditation verses of any God(dess) describe the form of that deity. This enables the devotees to imagine the form of the divinity while praying. Normally any Deity is formless (*niroopa*) and *nirguna* (without any specific character). Still since we are not yet matured to meditate upon the Deity without form, the meditation verses explain the image of the deities in one or other forms.

As per meditation verses of *Vatuka Bhairava*, he comprises all the three *gunas* together (*saguna*) and also separately as *Vatuka* in *sāttvik*, *rājasik* and *tāmasik* guises. In his form as the three gunas, he is described as being like pure crystal, effulgent as the rays from 1,000 Suns, shining like a sapphire thundercloud and wearing sapphire coloured clothing. He has three eyes, eight armed or four armed or two armed, depending on the preponderance of the *guna*, has a fanged, fearsome gaping mouth and a girdle and anklets of live snakes. He is *digambara* (naked as space), He is the prince-lord (*Kumaresha*) and is very powerful. In his right hands he holds a staff with a skull on the top (*khatvanga*), a sword, a noose and a trident. His left hands hold the hourglass-shaped *damaru* drum, a skull (probably that of *Brahma*). He shows the hand-sign bestowing boons and holds a snake in the last.

The *sāttvik dhyana* describes *Bhairava* as resembling crystal and as white as the *kunda* flower, wearing celestial clothing and nine gems, of a flaming appearance, adorned with anklets of bells, having a bright, beautiful and handsome face, with three eyes. He has two hands, one of which wields a trident (*shoola*).

The *rājasik dhyana* verse describes that he resembles the rising sun, with three eyes, with red limbs, in his four hands showing the sign bestowing boons and holding a skull. In one of his left hands, he holds a trident and with the other shows the hand gesture, dispelling fear. He has a blue, bejeweled throat, on his forehead is a fragment (*kala*) of the crescent moon red as the *banduka* flower and he wears clothes.

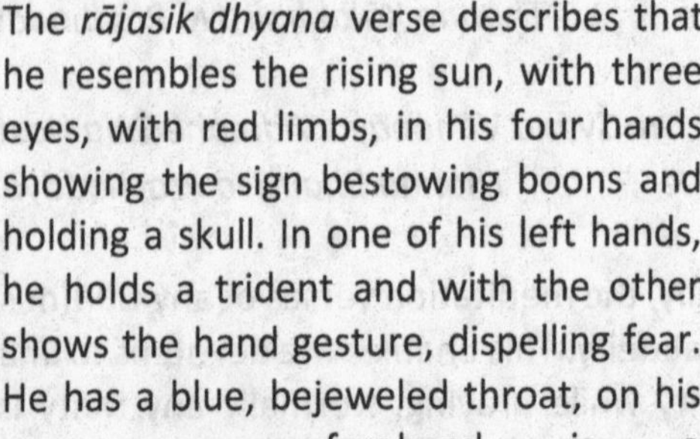

The last, *tamasik* dhyana hymn explains, *Bhairava* as stark naked, blue in colour, with reddened hair, with terrifying fangs, three eyes, anklets of jingling bells, and with eight arms.

The skull of Brahma also called as Brahma Kapala got stuck to his hand and this is depicted in the iconographic image of Lord *Kāla Bhairava* found in all temples. *Kāla Bhairaav*'s vehicle or *vahana* is a black dog. *Kāla Bhairava* appears naked like a child and wanders like a mendicant.

Though appearing fearful, *Kāla* Bhairava is a highly benevolent form of Lord Shiva. He is depicted in an aggressive form with angry eyes shaped like lotus blossoms, blazing hair, tiger's teeth, snake coiled around his neck or crown and an eerie garland of human skulls. Often terrifying, *Kāla* Bhairava carries a trident, a drum and the severed fifth head of Brahma. The deity is blue throated from swallowing poison to save the world. Hence, he is considered to be the vanquisher of death. His third eye represents eternal supreme wisdom.

Kala Bhairava is one of the eight Bharaiva fierce manifestations of Lord Shiva. He is blue-throated. He is three-eyed with eternal supreme wisdom in his third eye. His eyes are like Lotus flowers. He is Death of death being the vanquisher of death. He is indestructible, wears the garland of human skulls and carries the trident.

Kāla Bhairava is the punisher, a ferocious avatar, who took form to ensure right was done. Of the many avatars of Lord Shiva, *Kāla* Bhairava is known to be the keeper of time just as his name suggests. He is also known as Lord Dandapani, i.e., the one wielding a stick to punish the offenders.

As per legends, Lord *Kāla* Bhairava took the form when an enraged Shiva wished to teach Lord Brahma a lesson. It so happened that the male Hindu trinity or Tridevs – Brahma, Vishnu and Mahesh aka Shiva got into an argument – who was the supreme most of all? Lord Shiva stated he was and therefore, Lord Vishnu backed out. However, Lord Brahma refused to quiet down.

It got to a point when sages and scholars had to intervene but Lord Brahma would not back out! Enraged, Lord Shiva took the form of *Kāla* Bhairava who, in his wrathful incarnation, astride a fearsome black dog, charged at Brahma and cutoff his fifth head.

Therefore, *Kāla* Bhairava helps to keep one's ego in check. As he cut off Brahma's head with his nail, the skull was stuck and is known as Brahma Kapala. This depiction is found in all Bhairava idols in India. He is kind and easily bestows his devotees with wealth and prosperity.

The word Kala suggests that he is the controller of time and the word Bhairava suggests that he is the most terrible form. Though his form is fearful, Lord KalaBhairava is highly merciful to his devotees and worshipping Him shall bestow several benefits. Let us all worship him and get benefitted.

Śrī Bhairava Mantras

Om Aim Hrām Klīm Śrī Bhairavāya Namaḥ

There are some interesting mantras to worship Bhairava Deva chanting which are said to remove fear, cure diseases, destroy enemies and bestow prosperity. A few of the chosen *mantras* to propitiate Bhairava Deva are given below. As mentioned earlier, these *mantras* per se and their usage, are got to be initiated by an appropriate Guru before start chanting them. They are mentioned only as a reference guide.

Pleasing *Kāla Bhairava* is very easy and can be easily done by chanting the *Kāla Bhairava mantras*. Once made a regular practice, *Kāla Bhairava mantras* can bestow infinite blessings upon the chanter and win him the divine blessings of the Lord leading to prosperity and the final salvation at the end. Therefore, people chant *Kāla Bhairava mantra* with great devotion and fervor.

Kāla Bhairava mantras are very powerful and effective most of big and powerful tantric and pandits use these *mantras*.

Bhairava Bheeja Mantras – The four syllables following *Om* are called *Bheejas* or seeds. These *bheejas* correspond to the sound form of Lord *Bhairava*.

"Om Aim Hrām Klīm Śrī Batuka Bhairavāya"

"Om Hrīm Batukāya Āpaduddhāraṇaya Kuru Kuru Batukāya Hrīm Om Namaḥ Śivāya"

"Om Hrām Hrīm Hrūm Hrīme Hroum Kṣam Kṣetrapālāya Kāla Bhairavāya Namaḥ"

Bhairava Gāyatri Mantras –

Om Kālakālāya Vidhmahey Kālāthīthāya Dhīmahi Thanno Kāla Bhairava Prachodhayāt.

Om Swarna Vijayaya Vidmahe Shoola Hastāya Dhīmahi Tanno Kāla Bhairava Prachodayāt

Om Shoola Hasthāya Vidmahe Svarna Varnāya Dhīmahi Tanno Bhairava Prachodayat.

Om Digambarāya Vidmahe Dhīrgatheekshnāya Dhīmahi Tanno Bhairava Prachodayath

Some more mantras specific to a particular type of Bhairava Devas or for specific result. This eleven *Bhairava mantras* are very powerful.

1.	Vatuka Bhairava	Om Hrīm Āpaduddharanāy Kuru Kuru Swāhā
2.	Swarnakarshana Bhairava	Om Shrīm Hrīm Klīm Om Namo Bhagavate Swarnākarshana Bhairavāya Hiranyam Dāpaya Daraya Shrīm Hrīm Klīm Swāhā
3.	Maha Bhairava Mantra	Om Bram Bhairavāya Namaḥ
4.	Pratyaksha Siddhi Vatuka Bhairava	Om Hrīm Vatukāya Āpaduddharanāya Kuru Kuru Vatukāya Namaḥ
5.	Dakshinonmukhi Bhairava Mantra	Om Bhram Bhram Bhram Bhairavāya Namaḥ
6.	Krodha Bhairava Mantra	Om Hum Hraum Ram Jwāl Karālyai Krodhashcha Krodha Bhairavāya Namaḥ
7.	Bhairava Mantra for Protection	Om Hrīm Bhairava Bhayankara Har Mām Raksha Raksha Hum Phat Swāhā
8.	Bhairava Mantra for Vasheekaran	Om Namo Vatuka Bhairavāya Kāmdevāya Yasya Yasya Drushyo Bhavāmi Yashcha Yash Cha Mām Sukham Tam Tam Mohayatu Swāhā

9.	*Bhairava Mantra* for Happy Life	*Om Hraum Hrīm Hroom Hlīm Hum Om*
10.	*Bhairava Mantra* for removal of all problems	*Om Klīm Vīm Room Dhrum Ghnīm Hrīm Vatuka Bhairavāya Namaḥ Swāhā*
11.	*Bhairava Mantra* used by Karna	*Om Bhram Bhram Bhram Krīm Bhram Bhram Bhram Phat*

How to chant *Bhairava Mantras* – To get the best result one should chant *Bhairava Mantras* early in the morning after taking bath and in front of God Bhairava Idol or picture. One should first possibly understand the meaning of the *Mantras* to maximize its effect.

Bhairava Mantra (The specified Mantra is to be recited for 108 times as a standard rule; however, changes if any will be mentioned by the priest at the time of the Pooja)

According to many gurus' devotees must chant the *beeja* syllables 8 times a day for a 1 minute each, anytime day or night. One can even chant the mantra more than 108 times or by writing 1,008 or 10,008 times for great outcomes and protection.

Chanting of Sri Kala Bhairava Gayatri Mantra Japam keeps the mind calm. Few minutes be watching Lord Bhairava picture or idol and then closing the eyes start reciting the Mantra[7] – 108 times in mind. Be fully concentrated while doing japa. If enough time is not available the counting can be reduced to 54/ 32 times. More than quantify, quality is important – the focus and attention are important than the number of times.

Those suffering from Navagraha Dosha (Surya Dosha, Chandra Dosha, Guja Dosha, Buddha Dosha, Guru Dosha, Shukra Dosha, Shani Dosha, Rahu Dosha, Kethu Dosha, Mangalya Dosha, Kalathra Dosha, Manglik Dosha, Naga Dosha, and Sarpa Dosha among others) can pray to Lord Bhairava by chanting the Bhairava

---

[7] Any mantra japam should be chant without moving the lips.

Gayatri Mantra and get benefited greatly as one can see the gradual improvement in the life.

Individuals who are suffering from the evil-effects of Lord Saturn's planetary transit (Shani), can pray to Lord Bhairava to subdue the evil effects. Praying to Lord Bhairava is also suggested for individuals suffering from Sade Sati Shani (7½ years of Shani), Janma Shani, Ashtama Shani, Ardha-Ashtama Shani, Shani Dasa and Shani Bhukthi.

Individuals who are suffering from ill-fate, bad health, enemies, jealousies, evil-eyes, unwanted competitions, curses, disturbances, problems-after-problems, hindrances, etc., can chant the Bhairava Gayatri Mantra and can see gradual improvement in life as Lord Bhairava will slowly dispel all these negativities and will bless the devotee with a peaceful life. Individuals that are suffering from nightmares, disturbances from evil-spirits, negative energies, spells, black magic, etc., can chant this mantra with full devotion to get rid from all these negativities.

Apart from that, individuals suffering from addictions like cigarette, alcohol, drug, gambling, sex and all other types of addictions will be able to get rid of their addictions by praying to Lord Bhairava by constantly chanting the Bhairava Gayatri Mantra with utmost devotion. Those who are in very severe medical conditions due to their addictions, the parents or the spouse or any other close relative, can chant the mantra on behalf by pronouncing the Name, Nakshatra (Birth Star), and Rasi (Moon Sign) before reciting the Gayatri Mantra of Lord Bhairava.

The Bhairava Gayatri Mantra can also be recited by those wishing to spend their time in a most progressive manner. Those who feel that they have wasted a lot of time on unproductive activities will benefit greatly by praying to Lord Bhairava.

Praying to Lord Bhairava before a journey will turn the journey into a fruitful and beneficial one. For those who are travelling alone, those feeling insecure while travelling, and all those travelling at night can chant the Bhairava Gayatri Mantra before undertaking your journeys. It is highly believed, that when Lord Bhairava is prayed with utmost devotion, one will be able to see a dog in a sudden manner while travelling (which many saints believe that it is Shvana, the vahana of Lord Bhairava).

Apart from that, when one has begotten the blessings and grace of Lord Bhairava by chanting the Bhairava Mantras such as the Bhairava Gayatri Mantra, he will constantly dream of a dog (sometime multiple dogs).

Also, all those whom are keeping dogs as their pets can pray to Lord Bhairava for the well-being, good health, and longevity of their pet dogs. Other animal and pet owners too can pray to Lord Bhairava for the well-being of their animals.

Best Days to Chant (If unable to chant daily) — Tuesdays, Wednesdays, Fridays, Krishna Paksha Ashtami thithi days, Amavasya (New Moon Day) and Pournami (Full Moon Day)

Best day for getting initiation of this Mantra — Krishna Paksha Ashtami thithi days (waning moon period), Amavasya (New Moon Day), and Purnima (Full Moon Day)

Best Time to Chant — During Sunrise or at midnight (when Lord Bhairava is prayed during midnight, it is believed that Goddess Bhairavi will also be present as well).

Number of Times to Chant — 9, 11, 108, or 1,008 times.

Who can chant this Mantra? Anyone regardless of gender, caste, age, etc.

How to worship? Either use idol or photo or yantra of Lord Bhairava.

To attain Mantra siddhi — 108 times for 45 days

Naivedya (food offerings) — Cashew nuts and/ or Punugu rice.

Flowers – Any fragrant flowers can be offered.

This mantra is to be chant sitting facing East.

Act of charity to please lord Bhairava – Feed stray dogs and quench their thirst. Scholars have mentioned that Lord Bhairava himself will come in the form of dogs during "Buddha Hora" to eat the food offered by his devotees.

<u>Ashta Bhairava</u> ("Eight Bhairavas") – Earlier itself it was mentioned about Ashta Bhairavas. All the Ashta Bhairava are manifestations of the Hindu Lord Bhairava. They guard and control the eight directions. Each Bhairava has eight sub Bhairavas under him. All of the Bhairavas are ruled and controlled by Maha Kala Bhairava, who is considered the supreme ruler of time of the universe and the chief form of Bhairava.

Ashta Bhairavas with their consort, vahana(mount), direction he guards are all given below. Also given the consecrated temples in Tamil Nadu, India, where people born on the listed nakshatras get his favours, thosha nivarthi (remedy for thosham) and their lucky stones (*Rāshi* gem stone).

Ashta Bhairavas, all 8 of them, can be seen at Kashi Vishwanath Temple, Sattainathar Temple, Sirkazhi and Aragalur Sri Kamanada Eswar Temple.

1. *Asitānga Bhairava*	
Consort	*Bhrāmi*
Vehicle	Swan
Form	Appears in golden hue, carries four weapons namely trishula, damaru, pasha and khadga (sword)
Colour	White
Direction	East
Star	Punarpoosam, Visakam, Poorattaadhi
Gem Stone	Puspharagham (Yellow Sapphire)

Temple	Sattanathar Temple, Sirkazhi and Brahma Sira Kandeeswarar Temple, Thirukandiyur.
Moola Mantram	*Om Hrīm, Hrām Hrīm Hrum Jam Klām Klīm Kloum Brāhmi Devi Sametaya Asithānga Bhairavāya Sarva Shāpa Nivarthithaya Om Hrīm Phat Swāhā*
Meaning of the *Mantra*	I bow down to Asitanga Bhairava who appears with mother Brahmi Devi and removes all curses.
Benefits of worshipping	Improves creative energy and brings success in all ventures.

2. *Ruru Bhairava*

Consort	Maheshwari
Vehicle	Ox (Rishabam)
Form	Appears in white colour with many ornaments decked with rubies. Carries akshamala, an goad (angusam), a book and a veena
Colour	Spatika colour
Direction	Southeast
Star	Karthikai, Uthiradam, Uthiram
Gem Stone	Manickam (Ruby)
Temple	Rathnagiriswarar Temple, Thirumarugal
Moola Mantram	*Om Hrīm, Śrīm Klīm Śrīm Śrīm Klīm Śrīm Sarvajana Vasīkaraya Sarva Jana Mohanāya Sarva Vaśyam Śīghram Śīghram Śrīm Klīm Śrīm Swāhā*
Meaning of the *Mantra*	I bow down to Ruru Bhairava, who can bring all people under his control. Let him bless me to win over people.
Benefits of worshipping	Helps conquer enemies and get people under one's control

3. *Chaṇḍa Bhairava*

Consort	*Koumāri*
Vehicle	Peacock
Form	Appears blue with a pleasant face. Carries Agni, shakti (spear), gada and kunda
Colour	Gold Colour
Direction	South

Star	Mirugasirisham, Chithirai, Avittam
Gem Stone	Pavazham (Coral)
Temple	Vaitheeswaran Koil
Moola Mantram	*Om Sarva Śakti Rūpāya Nīla Varnāya Mahā Chaṇḍa Bhairavāya Namaḥ*
Meaning of the *Mantra*	I bow down to Chanda Bhairava who is blue in colour and the repository of all powers.
Benefits of worshipping	Gives the highest self-confidence and helps overcome competitions and enemies

<h3 style="text-align:center">4. Krodha Bhairava</h3>

Consort	*Vaiṣṇavī*
Vehicle	Eagle (Garuda)
Form	Appears grey in colour and carries khetaka, a long sword and axe.
Colour	Black
Direction	South-West
Star	Rohini, Hastham, Tiruvonam
Gem Stone	Muthu (Pearl)
Temple	Thiruvisanallur, Thirunaraiyur
Moola Mantram	*Om Śrīm Hrīm, Śrīm Hrīm Klīm Sarva Vighna Nivaraṇāya Mahā Krodha Bhairavāya Namaḥ*
Meaning of the *Mantra*	I bow down to Maha Krodha Bairav who removes all obstacles.
Benefits of worshipping	Gives the power to make potential and crucial decisions in life.

<h3 style="text-align:center">5. Unmattha Bhairava</h3>

Consort	*Vārahi*
Vehicle	Horse
Form	Appears in white colour with a pleasing face carrying *kunda*, the *khetaka*, the *parigha* (iron bludgeon) and *bhindipala* (javelin)
Colour	Gold Colour
Direction	West
Star	
Gem Stone	
Temple	Thiruveezhimizhalai
Moola Mantram	*Om Hrīm, Vārāhi Samethāya Mahā Unmattha Bhairavāya Hrīm Om Swāha*

Meaning of the *Mantra*	I bow down to Unmattha Bhairava who appears with mother Varahi. Let him bless me with a powerful speech.
Benefits of worshipping	Help gain control over your speech and blesses with an eloquent speech.

6. *Kapāla Bhairava*

Consort	Indrani
Vehicle	Elephant
Form	Yellow in complexion, carries the same weapons like that of Unmatta Bhairava
Colour	Blue Sapphire
Direction	North-West
Star	Bharani, Pooram, Pooradam
Gem Stone	*Vairam* (Diamond)
Temple	Thiruvirkudi, Thirupanthuruthi
Moola Mantram	*Om Hrīm Krīm Hrīm Klīm Śrīm Klīm Śrīm Kapāla Bairavāya Namaḥ*
Meaning of the *Mantra*	I bow down to Kapala Bhairava and seek his blessings.
Benefits of worshipping	Puts an end to all unproductive works and actions.

7. *Bhīṣaṇa Bhairava*

Consort	*Chāmuṇḍi*
Vehicle	Lion
Form	Appears red in colour and carries the weapons same as those of Unmatta Bhairava
Colour	Red
Direction	North
Star	Thiruvadhirai, Swati, Sadayam, Ashwini, Magha, Moola
Gem Stone	
Temple	Rameswaram, Piranmalai
Moola Mantram	*Om Hrīm Mahā Bhīṣaṇa Bhairavāya Sarva Śābha Nivāranaya Mama Vaśam Kuru Kuru Swāhā*
Meaning of the *Mantra*	I bow down to *Bhīshana Bhairava* who removes all curses and evil spells. May I be

	heled to conquer the evil spirits and negative forces.
Benefits of worshipping	Helps conquer all evil spirits and negativity

8. *Samhāra Bhairava*

Consort	*Caṇḍī*
Vehicle	Dog
Form	Appears like lightening and carries the weapons same as those of Unmattha Bhairava
Colour	White
Direction	North-East
Star	Ayilyam, Ketai, Revathi
Gem Stone	
Temple	Thiruvenkadu, Kolli Malai, Vairavanpatti, Hosur
Moola Mantram	*Om Hrīm, Hrām Hrīm Hrūm Jam Klām Klīm Kloum Caṇḍi Devi Sametaya Samhāra Bhairavāya Sarva Shāpa Nivarthithaya Om Hrīm Phat Swāhā*
Meaning of the *Mantra*	I bow down to Samhara Bhairava, who vanquishes all evils like ghosts, devils, demons and others. Let him help me overcome all negative forces.
Benefits of worshipping	Helps in dissolving all the bad consequences of past actions.

According to Hindu Mythology regularly chanting of Bhairava Mantras, is the most powerful and easy way to please Bhairava and God get his blessings.

Regular chanting of Mantra gives peace of mind and keeps away all the evils and makes the life healthy, wealthy and prosperous.

Thus, this fearful manifestation of Lord Shiva is believed to be one of the most protective powers blessing for humanity.

Śrī Bhairava Yantram

It is usual to worship Gods through *mantras*, *tantras* and *yantras*. Worshipping through *mantras* is called Māntrīka method. Worshipping through *tantras* is called Tāntrīka method. Worshipping through *yantras* is called Vaidhīka method. Whichever be the method *mantras* are definitely used to worship. But which is the main one is to be considered.

Mantras, the sound form of deities, are integral to *Sādhanas* (worship). *Mantra* each God/ Goddess will have different number of letters called *chandas*. Similarly, each God/ Goddess will have various *mantras* – probably each one for a particular purpose/ satiating a desire.

Tantras (Looms or Weavings) refer to numerous and varied scriptures pertaining to any of several esoteric traditions rooted in philosophy of the religion. The religious culture of the *Tantras* is essentially *Tāntric* material can be shown to have been derived from earlier *Vedic* sources. And although *Tantras* of different religions have many similarities from the outside, they do have some clear distinctions.

Yantras are some mathematical drawings/ patterns used for worship. There are mathematical construction methods explaining the drawing of *yantras*. *Yantras* mean originally the mechanical, mnemonic and musical contraption in the macrocosm. It is a graphic symbol of the contemplative meditation in the tradition, which was intended to be unified with the Gods/ goddesses. *Yantras* area also called as *cakras*. In a human body itself we have seven cakras thought to be an energy point or node in the subtle body viz., *Mūlādhārā*, *Swādhiṣṭānā*, *Maṇipūrakā*, *Anāhatā*, *Viśuddha*, *Agjnā* and *Sahasrārā*.

Usually when consecrating an idol of a deity, it is customary to place the yantras of the respective deities beneath the respective idols, duly drawn on copper, five-metals, silver, gold, etc. Properly drawn yantras emit micro-vibrations. Those vibrations are not feelable by human beings. However, they have a huge impact on our body, mainly positive impact. It is customary to worship the concerned deity alongwith the respective chakras/ yantras.

Yantras are great cosmic conductors of energy, an antenna of Nature, a powerful tool for harmony, prosperity, success, good health, yoga and meditation. Yantras are usually made out of copper and consist of a series of geometric patterns. The eyes and mind concentrate at the center of the yantra to achieve higher levels of consciousness.

There are lots of variances in the yantras pertaining to Lord Bhairava. The yantra of Bhairava, in all his different forms, is similar to that shown below.

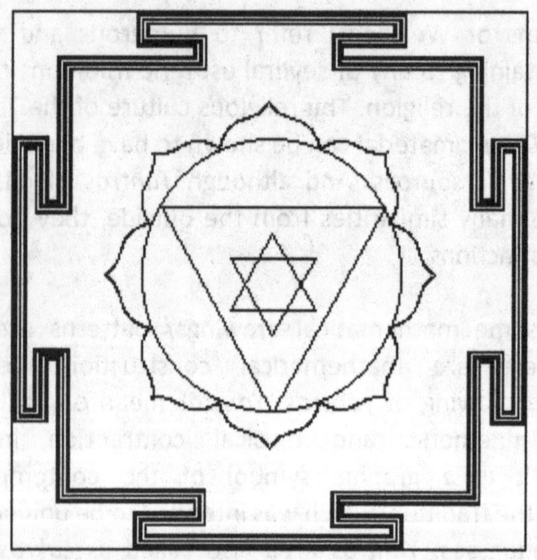

This Bhairava Yantra is also called as Bhairava Chakra or *Ādhi* (earliest) *Bhairava Chakra*.

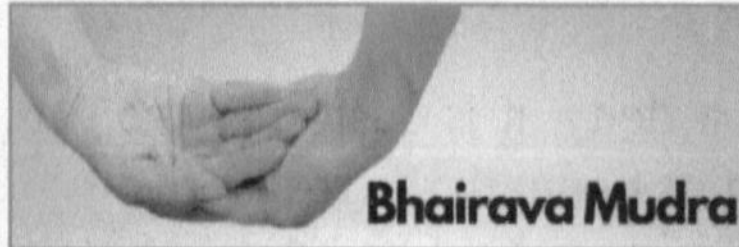

From the yogic point of view, if an individual applies the Bhairava Mudra, he or she looks both outwards and inwards at the same time and is one with Shiva-Shakti. Bhairava is terrible, terrifying, because he represents pure consciousness, before which the kleshas (obstacles) and conditioning of an ignorant human being crumble. The Netra Tantra text reveals more of the mysteries of Bhairava.

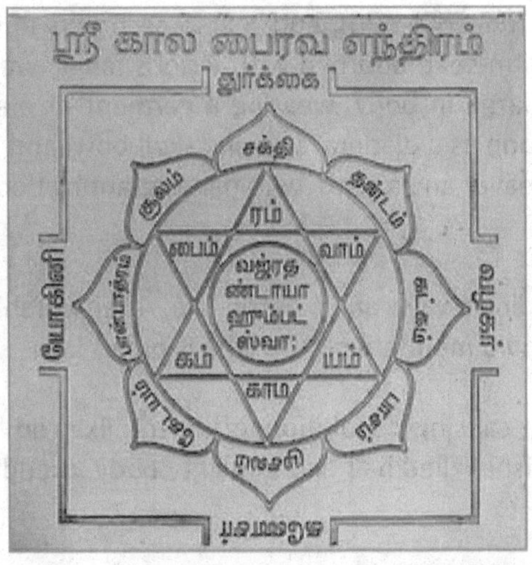

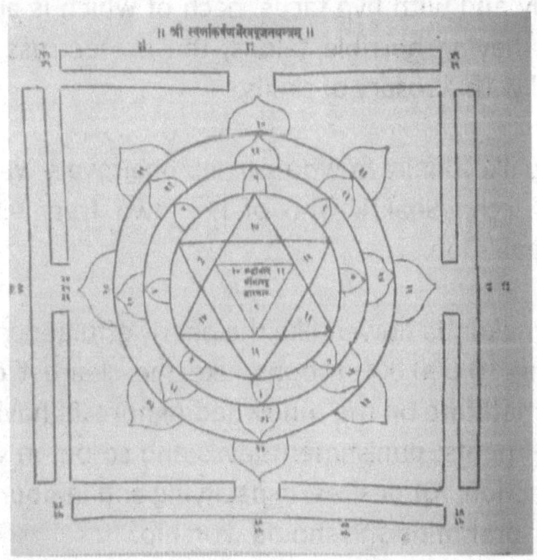

In Bhairava Yamala Tantra text, Lord Shiva speaks of the characteristics of the Bhairava Agama, resembling a mass of fragments of collyrium, like the fire at the end of an aeon.

Five faced, seated on a corpse, with ten arms, the dispeller of anxiety, resembling a host of night flowers, the final peal of thunder, making a terrifying roar.

Having a gaping fanged mouth, and fearsome brows and eyes, enthroned on a lion-seat, adorned with vicious fangs, wearing a rosary of skulls, large in body, wearing a garment of elephant-hide, with the Moon as a diadem, carrying skull-bowl and a skull-staff, bearing a cleaver and a goad, with hands granting boons and dispelling fears.

A great hero, holding a vajra and a battle-axe. After worshipping Bhairava, one should meditate on she who is on his lap.

Similar to the fire causing dissolution, effulgent, like red lac and vermilion, with dishevelled hair and a mighty body, dreadful and truly terrific.

With a great belly and with five faces, each of which is adorned with three eyes, having horrible talons, the protectress of the fortress, adorned with a rosary of skulls.

A Devi with arms like Bhairava who carries Bhairava's weapons, thus is declared Iccha Shakti, who of her own free will goes lovingly on Bhairava's lap.

Resembling a Hemakunda flower, like the pearly effulgence of the Moon, resembling 10,000,000 Moons, like the clearest crystal, thus should one meditate on the renowned Aghoreshi having the above form. In ailments, punishment, evils and so on, in various setbacks, in protection, for desires, in pacifying and in nourishing, for cowns and for brahmins one should worship.

(Chit Bhairava) is like the fire at the end of the aeon, red as the China rose, equivalent to 10,000,000 Suns. One should meditate on him as red or blackish in hue. Effulgent as a red lotus or like yellow orpiment, being of the nature of Will (Iccha), the deva bestowing the fruit of Icchasiddha.

One should meditate on (these forms) placed in the centre of a lotus and should worship, according to the ritual injunction with food, flower, incense and distilled liquor abundantly. The Devi resembling cow's milk, effulgent as a necklace of pearls like beautiful pure crystal, white as snow, pure as camphor, with four arms and one face adorned with three eyes. The Devi wearing white garments, ornamented with white pearls, seated on a deer with a vajra in her hand, very powerful, the (Siddha Devi).

Hence, in the four directions are situated the Devis of Bhairava, O Mother of Hosts! In the intermediate points are placed the Dutis, the south east being first and the north east last. Kali, Karali, Mahakali and Bhadrakali are the renowed Devis placed there. The Devis have two arms and sit on a lotus, carrying a knife and a severed head. The attendants of the door are Krodhana, Vrintaka, Karshana and Gajanana, with two arms, of deformed appearance and holding a cleaver and a shield. In the matter of pacifying acts, they are all-white, or in other acts according to their forms.

Now I declare the characteristics of the Rajaraksha. By the yoga of enveloping in a mantra, one should write the name in the centre.

Above this, one should worship the lord of nectar, who is Bhairava, dear one. Similarly, the Devis should be worshipped in the petals of the lotus.

Afterwards, one should worship the Dutis and the servants using the root mantra. On the outside of the lotus one should draw a very white Moon mandala. On the outside of this is a bhupura, marked with the vajra symbol. Having drawn it using rochana, kumkum or white milk, one should worship, in pacifying acts, using all-white ritual accessories, giving suitable food, and animal sacrifice of vicious beasts of prey.

The wise man should do homa using white sandal, mixed with camphor and ash, unhusked rice, sesame oil together with white sugar, ghee and milk. Great peace comes swiftly by worshipping the Mrityunjaya.

Thus Lord Bhairava and his Devi have to imagined in his Yantra and worshipped, says Lord Shiva.

Kalabhairava is the Lord of Time who can bless with effective time management skills, as well as relieve from debts. When one owes volumes of debts and struggle to balance the time, seek the divine help of Kalabhairava. Offering sincere prayers to his Yantra can nullify the debts and amplify the sources of income.

The Yantra emits powerful vibrations that can gift with the skill of handling time efficiently. With the Yantra of Kalabhairava one can master the art of multitasking and stay ahead of time!

Śrī Bhairava Pooja

In general, *Bhairava* Puja Procedure is rather severe and elaborate. However, the Puja Procedure in brief is narrated below. Readers are requested to get in touch with an appropriate guru before starting the puja.

The purpose of Bhairava Pooja –

Time and tide wait for none goes the saying. Controlling time and maintaining punctuality is a lacking birth quality for many. Kala Bhairava blesses his devotees with the power of controlling the factors called time and incidents that take place in the life. He is so easily pleased and blesses his devotees with wealth, health and prosperity.

Bhairava Puja Procedure in Brief

Keep a *Shrī Bhairava Yantra* of a picture or idol of *Shrī Bhairava* in front and Coconut, Flowers, Sindoor, Mustard oil, black til, etc., should be offered. The root mantra has to be chant. Liquor, honey to replace alcohol, is also offered. During the mantra sadhana it is essential to eat only once a day, observe celibacy and sleep only on the ground. Mantra is to be repeated 1,25,000 times to obtain the complete blessings of lord Bhairav.

Shri Bhairava Moola Mantra –

Om Śrīm Klīm Śrīm Swarṇapradāyai Namaḥ Śrīm Klīm Śrīm

Ganapati Puja and Punyahavacanam

शुक्लाम्बरधरं विष्णुं शशिवर्णं चतुर्भुजम् ।
प्रसन्नवदनं ध्यायेच्च सर्वविघ्नोपशान्तये ॥
Shukla-Ambara-Dharam Vishnum Shashi-Varnam Catur-
Bhujam |
Prasanna-Vadanam Dhyaayet Sarva-Vighno Upashaantaye |

Pranayamam (gents only)

*Sankalpam - Mamopatha Samastha, Duritha kshaya dwara,
Sri Parameshwara Preethyartham, Sri Vijaya Bhairava
Preethyartham, Sri Vijaya Bhairava Prasada Sidyartham*
<description of the concerned location>
<description of the relevant day>
<description of gotra, star and rashi of the family members>
<purpose for which the puja is performed>
Sri Vijaya Bhairava pujaam karishye ॥

Bell Puja
Asana Puja
Kalasa Puja

ॐ पारिजात द्रुम कान्तारुस्तितभ्राणिक्य मण्ढपे |

सिम्हासन घतं वन्दभ्रैरवं स्वर्ण धायकम् ॥

काङ्कक्ष पात्रं ढमरूं त्रिशूलं वरं कर: सन्ततं त्रिनभ्रम् |

धभ्रमायुदं तभ स्वर्ण वर्ण स्वर्णाकर्षण भैरवं आश्रयामि ॥

*Om Pārijāta Druma Kāntārē Stitē Māṇikya Maṇṭapē |
Simhāsaṇa Gatam Vandē Bhairavam Svarṇa Dhāyakam ॥
Kāṅkēya Pātram Ḍamarūm Triśūlam Varam Karaḥ Santatam
Trinētram |
Dēvyāyudam Tapta Svarṇa Varṇa Svarṇākarṣaṇa Bhairavam
Āśrayāmi ॥
Om Srī Vijaya Bhairavam Dhyāyāmi ॥*

ॐ एं ऐं क्लीं ग्लूं हां हीं हूं हैं हौं ह: आपदुद्धारणाय अजमल वद्धाय
लोकश्वराय स्वर्णाकर्षण भैरवाय मम धारिद्रिय द्वंशनाय दनाकर्षण
सिद्धिदाय ॐ श्री महा स्वर्णाकर्षण भैरवाय नम: ॥

*Om Ēm Aim Klīm Glūm Hrām Hrīm Hrūm Hraim Hroum Hraḥ
Āpaduddhāraṇāya Ajāmala Vaddhāya Lōkēśvarāya
Svarṇākarṣaṇa Bhairavāya Mama Dhāridriya Dvamśaṇāya
Daṇākarṣaṇa Siddhidāya Om Śrī Mahā Svarṇākarṣaṇa
Bhairavāya Namaḥ ॥*

Om Srī Vijaya Bhairavam Āvāhayāmi ||

Prāṇa Pratiṣṭai

Om Srī Vijaya Bhairavāya Namaḥ Pratiṣṭāpayāmi ||

Prāṇa Pratiṣṭa Kālē ______ Nivētayāmi ||

Āsanam

नानारत्न समायुक्तं कार्तस्वर विभूषितम् ।
आसनं देवदेवेश प्रीत्यर्थं प्रतिगृह्यताम् ॥

Nānāratṇa Samāyuktam Kārtasvara Vibhūṣitam |

Āsaṇam Dēvadēvēśa Prītyartham Pratigruhyatām ||

Om Srī Vijaya Bhairavāya Namaḥ Ratna Simhāsanam

Samarpayāmi ||

Pādyam

गंगादिसर्वतीर्थेभ्य: मया प्रार्थनया हृतम् ।
तोयमेतत्सुखस्पर्श सौख्यार्थ प्रतिगृह्यताम् ॥

Gaṅgādi Sarva Tīrthēbhyaḥ Mayā Prārthanayā Hrutam |

Tōyamētat Sukhasparśam Saukhyārtham Prati Gruhyatām ||

Om Srī Vijaya Bhairavāya Namaḥ Pādayōḥ Gandākṣata Sahita

Pādyam Samarpayāmi ||

Arghyam

नमस्ते देवदेवेश नमस्ते धरणीधर ।
नमस्ते सर्वविनुत गृहाणार्घ्यं नमोऽस्तु ते॥

Namastē Dēvadēvēśa Namastē Dharaṇīdhara |

Namastē Sarvavinuta Gruhāṇārghyam Namōstu Tē ||

Om Srī Vijaya Bhairavāya Namaḥ Hastayōḥ Gandākṣata Puṣpa

Sahita Arghyam Samarpayāmi ||

Ācamaṇīyam

कर्पूर वासितं तोयं गङ्गादिभ्य: समाहृतम् ।
आचम्यतां जगन्नाथ मया दत्तं हि भक्तित: ॥

Karpūra Vāsitam Tōyam Gaṅgādibhyaḥ Samāhrutam |

Ācamyatām Jagannātha Mayā Dattam Hi Phaktitaḥ ||

          Om Srī Vijaya Bhairavāya Namaḥ Mukhē Ācamaṇīyam

                              Samarpayāmi ||

Snāṉam

गङ्गा च यमुना चैव नर्मदा च सरस्वती ।
कृष्णा गोदावरी वेणी क्षिप्रा सिन्धुर्घटप्रभा ॥
तापि पयोष्णी सरयूस्ताभ्य: स्नानार्थमाहतम् ।
तोयमन्नत्सुखस्पर्शं सुगन्धि प्रतिगृह्यताम् ॥

Gaṅgā Ca Yamuṉā Caiva Narmadā Ca Sarasvatī |

Kruṣṉā Gōdāvarī Vēṇī Kṣiprā Sindhurghaṭaprabhā ||

Tāpi Payōṣṇī Sarayūstābhyaḥ Snānārthamāhrutam |

Tōyamētatsukhasparśam Sugandhi Pratgruhyatām ||

          Om Srī Vijaya Bhairavāya Namaḥ Śuddhōdaka Snāṉam

                              Samarpayāmi ||

                    Snāṉantaram Ācamaṇīyam Samarpayāmi ||

Vastram

सर्वभूषाधिकक्षसौंय्यत्रोकलज्जानिवारणभ्र
वाससी प्रतिगृह्यत्राां मया तुभ्यं समर्पितभ्र

Sarvabhūṣādhikē Saumyē Lōkalajjānivāraṇē |

Vāsasī Pratgruhyētām Mayā Tubhyam Samarpitē ||

          Om Srī Vijaya Bhairavāya Namaḥ Vastram Samarpayāmi ||

      Om Srī Vijaya Bhairavāya Namaḥ Yagnopavīam Samarpayāmi ||

       Om Srī Vijaya Bhairavāya Namaḥ Ābharaṇāṉi Samarpayāmi ||

Sandal Paste (*Gandham*)

श्रीखण्डचन्दनं दिव्यं गन्धाढ्यं सुमनोहरम् ।
विलेपनं सुरश्रेष्ठ प्रीत्यर्तं प्रतिगृह्यताम् ॥

Śrīkhaṇḍacandanam Divyam Gandhāḍhyam Sumanōharam |
Vilēpanam Suraśrēṣṭa Prītyartam Pratigruhyatām ||

Om Srī Vijaya Bhairavāya Namaḥ Śītāṉa Gandhāṉ
Samarpayāmi ||

Om Srī Vijaya Bhairavāya Namaḥ Gandasya Upari Haridrā
Kuṅkumam Samarpayāmi ||

Akṣatāḥ

अक्षतानक्षतान् दिव्यान् कुङ्कुमाक्तान् सुशोभनान् ।
मया निवेदितान् भक्त्या गृहाण परमेश्वर ॥

Akṣatānakṣatāṉ Divyāṉ Kuṅkumāktāṉ Suśōbhanāṉ |
Mayā Nivēditāṉ Bhaktyā Gruhāṇa Paramēśvara ||

Om Srī Vijaya Bhairavāya Namaḥ Haridrā Akṣatāṉ
Samarpayāmi ||

Puṣpamālā

पुष्पाणि च सुगन्धीनि मालत्यादीनि च प्रभो ।
मयाऽऽहृतानि पूजार्थं पुष्पाणि प्रतिगृह्यताम् ॥

Puṣpāṇi Ca Sugandhīni Mālatyādīni Ca Prabhō |
Mayā́hrutāni Pūjārtham Puṣpāṇi Pratigruhyatām ||

Om Srī Vijaya Bhairavāya Namaḥ Puṣpamālāṉ Samarpayāmi ||

Arcaṇa

1.	ॐ स्वर्णप्रदाय नम:		Om Svarṇapradāya Namaḥ.
2.	ॐ स्वर्णवर्शाय नम:		Om Svarṇavarṣāya Namaḥ.
3.	ॐ स्वर्णाकिर्षणाय नम:		Om Svarṇākarṣaṇāya Namaḥ.
4.	ॐ बक्तप्रिय नम:		Om Baktapriyāya Namaḥ.
5.	ॐ बक्तवश्य नम:		Om Baktavaśyāya Namaḥ.
6.	ॐ बक्ताभीष्ट फलप्रदाय नम:		Om Baktāpīṣṭa Palapratāya Namaḥ.
7.	ॐ सिद्धिदाय नम:		Om Siddhitāya Namaḥ.
8.	ॐ करुणामूर्तयभ्रम:		Om Karuṇāmūrtayē Namaḥ.
9.	ॐ बक्ताभीष्ट प्रपूरकाय नम:		Om Baktābhīṣṭa Prapūrakāya Namaḥ.
10.	ॐ निदिसिद्धिप्रदाय नम:		Om Nidisiddhipratāya Namaḥ.
11.	ॐ स्वर्णासिद्धिदाय नम:		Om Svarṇāsiddhitāya Namaḥ.
12.	ॐ रससिद्धिदाय नम:		Om Rasasiddhitāya Namaḥ.

Om Srī Vijaya Bhairavāya Namaḥ Puṣpaiḥ Sampoojayāmi ॥

Srī Bhairava Deva arcana can be done with the above 12 or the 108 or 1,008 names given in other chapters of this book, depending on the time and materials available.

Dhoopaḥ

दशाङ्गो गुग्गुलूपन्न: सुगन्ध: सुमनोहर: |
आघ्रन्न: सर्वदन्त्रानां धूपोऽयं प्रति गृह्यताम् ॥

Daśāṅgō Guggulūpētaḥ Sugandhaḥ Sumanōharaḥ |

Āghrēyaḥ Sarva Dēvānām Dhūpōyam Prati Gruhyatām ||

Om Srī Vijaya Bhairavāya Namaḥ Dhoopam Āgrāpayāmi ||

Dhoopānantaram Ācamanīyam Samarpayāmi ||

Dheepaḥ

साज्यं त्रिवर्ति संयुक्तं वह्निना योजितं मया ।

गृहाण मङ्गलं दीपं त्रैलोक्यतिमिरापहम् ॥

Sājyam Trivarti Samyuktam Vahninā Yōjitam Mayā |

Gruhāṇa Maṅgalam Dīpam Trailōkyatimirāpaham ||

Om Srī Vijaya Bhairavāya Namaḥ Dheepam Dariśayāmi ||

Dheepānantaram Ācamanīyam Samarpayāmi ||

Mahānaivēdyam

Om Srī Vijaya Bhairavāya Namaḥ Idam Sarvam Nivēdayāmi |

Nivēdayānantaram Ācamanīyam Samarpayāmi ||

Madhyē Madhyē Pānīyam Samarpayāmi ||

Hastaprakṣāḷanam Samarpayāmi ||

Pātaprakṣāḷanam Samarpayāmi ||

Punaḥ Ācamanīyam Samarpayāmi ||

Karpūra Tāmbūlam

पूगीफल समायुक्तं नागवल्लीदलैर्युतम् ।

कर्पूरचूर्ण संयुक्तं ताम्बूलं प्रतिगृह्यताम् ॥

Pūgīphala Samāyuktam Nāgavallīdalairyutam |

Karpūracūrṇa Samyuktam Tāmbūlam Pratigruhyatām ||

Om Srī Vijaya Bhairavāya Namaḥ Karpūra Tāmbūlam

Samarpayāmi || Samastopacārān samarpayāmi ||

Nīrājaṇam (Kaṟpūram)

*Om Bhairavāya Vidhmahē Harihara Brahmātmakāya Dhīmahi
Taṇṇaḥ Svarṇākarṣaṇa Bhairavaḥ Pracōdayāt ॥*

*Om Srī Vijaya Bhairavāya Namaḥ Samasta Pāpakṣayārtam,
Sarva Maṅgala Avāptyarttam Kaṟpūra Nīrāja Deepam
Sandarśayāmi ॥
Nīrājaṇāṇantaram Ācamaṇīyam Samarpayāmi ॥
Divya Rakṣāṇ Dārayāmi ॥*

Mantra Puṣpam

*Yōpām Puṣpam Vēdā.....
Om Srī Vijaya Bhairavāya Namaḥ Vēdōkta Mantra Puṣpāñcalīm
Samarppayāmi ॥
Svarṇa Puṣpa Dakṣiṇāṇ Samarppayāmi ॥*

Pradakṣiṇa Namaskārāḥ

ॐ श्रीं ग्लीं श्रीं नमो बगवते विजय भैरवाय प्राणादाभीष्ट तत्पर पूरणाय
एहि एहि करुणानिधध्रमहां हिरण्य सिद्धिञ्च तापय तापय
शीग्रं श्रीं ग्लीं श्रीं नम: ॥
ॐ नमो बगवतभ्रविजय भैरवाय धन धान्य विरुद्धिकराय
शीग्रं स्वर्ण धच्चि धच्चि वश्यम् कुरुकुरु नम: ॥
ॐ नमस्तभ्रैरवाय ब्रह्म विष्णु शिवात्मनभ्राम:
त्रैलोक्य वन्द्याय वरधाय वरात्मनभ्रा

*Om Śrīm Klīm Śrīm Namō Bhagavatē Vijaya Bhairavāya
Prāṇādhābīṣṭa Tatpara Pūraṇāya Ēhi Ēhi Karuṇāṇidē
Mahyam Hiraṇya Siddhiñca Tāpaya Tāpaya Śīkram Śrīm Klīm
Śrīm Namaḥ ॥*

*Om Namō Bhagavatē Vijaya Bhairavāya Daṇa Dāṇya
Viruddhikarāya Śīkram Svarṇam Dēhi Dēhi Vaśyam Kurukuru
Namaḥ ॥*

*Om Namastē Bhairavāya Brahma Viṣṇu Śivātmaṇē Namaḥ
Trailōkya Vandyāya Varadāya Varātmaṇē ॥*

Om Srī Vijaya Bhairavāya Namaḥ Aṉantakōṭi Pradakṣiṇa Namaskārāṉ Samarppayāmi ||

Prārtaṉāṉi Samarpayāmi ||

Samastōpacāraṉ Śaktyōpacāraṉ Śōḍaśōpacāraṉ Samarppayāmi ||

Anayā Pūjayāḥ Śrī Vijaya Bhairava Deva Prīyatām ||

Om Tat Sat ||

*****

Śrī Bhairava Deva Homa

Om Hrīm Vijaya Bhairavāya Namaḥ

Homam or havan is the practice of chanting various mantras about a particular God or Gods and offering in the sacred fire. This has been practiced by the ancient Rishis since Vedic times. Homam has been practiced as an important religious ritual in Hinduism. It is an integral part of most cultures. Although there are some minor differences, nowadays, Homam, Havan, Yajna, Agnihotram, all speak in the same sense.

General homa procedures – in brief –

Fill a kumbha (pot – usually of copper or brass or silver) with water, invoke Varuna (Lord of water) and the respective deities. Invoke and worship the respective deities in the Homa fire and then perform the Homa with the root mantra. Homam should be done after performing ten times more japam/ chanting (*dhashamsa*) than the number of homams performed with the mantra. For instance, if 100 times japam is made then 10 times homa has to be performed.

At the end the power of God in the holy fire is transferred to the kumbha (pot) and further puja is performed. Then the holy water in the pot is sprinkled on the idol. Koorcham made of Dharba grass, coconut and mango leaves kept on the kumbha touching the water inside, act as antennae, grasp the mantras chant and make the water holy.

Some Highlights of Kala Bhairava Homam –

Time is of the essence. In this modern age, for those of us who are running in a hurry, Bhairava Homam is capable of giving the ability to manage this glorious period well. The energy that emanates from this homam can make us realize the value of every moment and teach us the timing of time. Through this homa, one can worship and satisfy the Bhairava and thereby gain the ability to complete the tasks easily and efficiently within the allotted time.

Significance of Kala Bhairava Homam –

Kala signifies 'time' and 'Bhairava' the appearance of Shiva. Performing Kala Bhairava Homam on all auspicious days, favours with time administration abilities, protects against mischances and other unforeseen occasions, brings sure vitality and achievement, eases from obligations and enhances budgetary status and frees negative Karma.

Time is the most important factor in the universe, and no one can reverse the effects of days gone by. Even Gods accept the inexorable march of time and respect its value. Time is money, thus managing it efficiently is vital for living a life with discipline and punctuality. Kala Bhairava Homam is performed to invoke the blessings of the deity to manage and utilize our time successfully for optimal results and productivity. It is of paramount significance for business people who seek to accomplish and attain success in their endeavours.

Traditional Homa Method –

காமியம் செய்து காலம் கழியாதே.
ஓமியம் செய்து உள்ளத் துணர்மினோ – (ஓமியம் = ஹோமம்).
(அப்பர் குறுந்தொகை – குடமூக்கு – 8)

By performing the Bhairava Homam, one seeks divine guidance in leading a life adhering to the principles of time management.

Kala Bhairava Homam is ideal for –

• To be blessed with a child
• People who are facing debts
• People who are not able to manage their time effectively
• People who are facing cramming in their life
• People who are facing difficulty in multi-tasking

Bhairava Homam should be conducted systematically with devotional zeal, as prescribed by Maharishis (sages), by experienced priests, who are well versed in the Vedic scriptures. Krishna Paksha Ashtami Day is considered to be the best day to perform this homam as it is the most auspicious day for Lord Bhairava. By participating in this, Homa one can receive the grace and excel in life.

Benefits of conducting Bhairava Homam –

- Improves time management skills
- Get protection from accidents and other unforeseen events
- Positive energy increases and the path to success develops
- The financial situation will improve
- Get rid of debts
- Get rid of sinful karmas
- Many of the skills will be improved

Bhairava Homa Mantras –

Om Swarṇa Vijayāya Vidmahe Śūla Hastāya Dhīmahi

Tanno Bhairava Pracodayāt ‖ Or

Om Hrīm Vijaya Bhairavāya Namaḥ ‖

Homam should be performed with samithu (sticks of pipal tree), puffed rice, nine grains (nava dhanyam), jaggery, sweets, ghee, spices, flowers, etc.

For Sri Vijaya Bhairava, who resides at the Srividya Ashram, Salem, Sri Vijaya Bhairava Homas are being held on all special days on behalf of the devotees. The devotees may participate in them and attain blissful prosperity. The devotees can also attend homas held at the Bhairava temples near their homes. Participating with devotion is important.

****

Śrī Aṣṭabhairava Dhyāna Stotram
अष्टभैरव ध्यानस्तोत्रम्

The word *Dhyāna* means to meditate upon. Normally any *Dhyāna* verse will describe the form of the corresponding God(dess). While chanting this verse, one has to imaging the God with focus, then definitely that God will appear in front of the devotee.

The meditative humns of the Ashta Bhairavs are given below both in English and Samskrutam.

Bhairavaḥ Pūrṇarūpohi Śaṅkarasya Parātmanaḥ |

Mūḍhāstevai Na Jānanti Mohitāḥ Śivamāyayā ||

Oṃ Haṃ Ṣaṃ Naṃ Gaṃ Kaṃ Saṃ Khaṃ Mahākālabhairavāya Namaḥ |

Namaskāra Mantraḥ || (to bow down)

Oṃ Śrībhairavyai, Oṃ Maṃ Mahābhairavyai, Oṃ Siṃ Siṃhabhairavyai, Oṃ Dhūṃ Dhūmrabhairavyai, Oṃ Bhīṃ Bhīmabhairavyai, Oṃ Uṃ Unmattabhairavyai, Oṃ Vaṃ Vaśīkaraṇabhairavyai, Oṃ Moṃ Mohanabhairavyai |

Aṣṭabhairava Dhyānam ||

Asitāṅgoruruścaṇḍaḥ Krodhaśconmattabhairavaḥ |

Kapālībhīṣaṇaścaiva Saṃhāraścāṣṭabhairavam ||

1) Asitāṅgabhairava Dhyānam |

Raktajvālajaṭādharaṃ Śaśiyutaṃ Raktāṅga Tejomayaṃ
Aste Śūlakapālapāśaḍamaruṃ Lokasya Rakṣākaram |
Nirvāṇaṃ Śunavāhanantrinayanamānandakolāhalaṃ
Vande Bhūtapiśācanātha Vaṭukaṃ Kṣetrasya Pālaṃ Śivam ||
2) Rūrubhairava Dhyānam |

Nirvāṇaṃ Nirvikalpaṃ Nirūpajamalaṃ Nirvikāraṃ Kṣakāraṃ
Huṅkāraṃ Vajradaṃṣṭraṃ Hutavahanayanaṃ

Raudramunmattabhāvam |

Bhaṭkāraṃ Bhaktanāgaṃ Bhṛkuṭitamukhaṃ Bhairavaṃ
Śūlapāṇiṃ Vande Khaḍgaṃ Kapālaṃ Ḍamarukasahitaṃ

Kṣetrapālannamāmi ||

3) *Caṇḍabhairava Dhyānam |*

Bibhrāṇaṃ Śubhravarṇaṃ Dviguṇadaśabhujaṃ
Pañcavaktrantrinetraṃ Dānañchatrenduhastaṃ
Rajatahimamṛtaṃ Śaṅkhabheṣasyacāpam |
Śūlaṃ Khaḍgañca Bāṇaṃ Ḍamarukasikatāvañcimālokya Mālāṃ
Sarvābhītiñca Dorbhīṃ Bhujatagiriyutaṃ Bhairavaṃ

Sarvasiddhim ||

4) *Krodhabhairava Dhyānam |*

Udyadbhāskararūpanibhantrinayanaṃ Raktāṅga Rāgāmbujaṃ
Bhasmādyaṃ Varadaṃ Kapālamabhayaṃ

Śūlandadhānaṃ Kare |

Nīlagrīvamudārabhūṣaṇaśataṃ Śanteśu Mūḍhojjvalaṃ
Bandhūkāruṇa Vāsa Astamabhayaṃ Devaṃ Sadā Bhāvayet

5) *Unmattabhairava Dhyānam |*

Ekaṃ Khaṭvāṅgahastaṃ Punarapi Bhujagaṃ Pāśamekantriśūlaṃ
Kapālaṃ Khaḍgahastaṃ Ḍamarukasahitaṃ Vāmahaste Pinākam
|
Candrārkaṃ Ketumālāṃ Vikṛtisukṛtinaṃ Sarvayajñopavītaṃ
Kālaṃ Kālāntakāraṃ Mama Bhayaharaṃ

Kṣetrapālannamāmi ||

6) *Kapālabhairava Dhyānam |*

Vande Bālaṃ Sphaṭikasadṛśaṃ Kumbhalollāsivaktraṃ
Divyākalpaiphaṇimaṇimayaikiṅkiṇīnūpurañca |
Divyākāraṃ Viśadavadanaṃ Suprasannaṃ Dvinetraṃ

Hastādyāṃ Vā Dadhānāntriśivamanibhayaṃ Vakradaṇḍau

Kapālam ||

7) *Bhīṣaṇabhairava Dhyānam* |

Trinetraṃ Raktavarṇañca Sarvābharaṇabhūṣitam |
Kapālaṃ Śūlahastañca Varadābhayapāṇinam ||
Savye Śūladharaṃ Bhīmaṃ Khaṭvāṅgaṃ Vāmakeśavam |
Raktavastraparidhānaṃ Raktamālyānulepanam |
Nīlagrīvañca Saumyañca Sarvābharaṇabhūṣitam ||
Nīlamekha Samākhyātaṃ Kūrcakeśantrinetrakam |
Nāgabhūṣañca Raudrañca Śiromālāvibhūṣitam ||
Nūpurasvanapādañca Sarpa Yajñopavītinam |
Kiṅkiṇīmālikā Bhūṣyaṃ Bhīmarūpaṃ Bhayāvaham ||

8) *Saṃhārabhairava Dhyānam* |

Ekavaktrantrinetrañca Hastayo Dvādaśantathā |
Ḍamaruñcāṅkuśaṃ Bāṇaṃ Khaḍgaṃ Śūlaṃ Bhayānvitam ||
Dhanurbāṇa Kapālañca Gadāgniṃ Varadantathā |
Vāmasavye Tu Pārśvena Āyudhānāṃ Vidhantathā ||
Nīlamekhasvarūpantu Nīlavastrottarīyakam |
Kastūryādi Nilepañca Śvetagandhākṣatantathā ||
Śvetārka Puṣpamālāñca Trikoṭyaṅgaṇasevitām |
Sarvālaṅkāra Saṃyuktāṃ Saṃhārañca Prakīrtitam ||

Iti Śrībhairava Stuti Nirudra Kurute |
Iti Aṣṭabhairava Dhyānastotraṃ Sampūrṇam |

भैरवः पूर्णरूपोहि शङ्करस्य परात्मनः |
मूढास्तत्त्रै न जानन्ति मोहिताः शिवमायया ||

ॐ हं षं नं गं कं सं खं महाकालभैरवाय नमः |

नमस्कार मन्त्रः |

ॐ श्रीभैरव्यै, ॐ मं महाभैरव्यै, ॐ सिं सिंहभैरव्यै,

ॐ धूं धूम्रभैरव्यै, ॐ भीं भीमभैरव्यै, ॐ उं उन्मत्तभैरव्यै,

ॐ वं वशीकरणभैरव्यै, ॐ मों मोहनभैरव्यै ।

अष्टभैरव ध्यानम् ॥

असिताङ्गोरुरुश्चण्डः क्रोधश्चोन्मत्तभैरवः ।

कपालीभीषणश्चैव संहारश्चाष्टभैरवम् ॥

१) असिताङ्गभैरव ध्यानम् ।

रक्तज्वालजटाधरं शशियुतं रक्ताङ्ग तन्त्रोमयं

अस्तभ्शूलकपालपाशडमरुं लोकस्य रक्षाकरम् ।

निर्वाणं शुनवाहनन्त्रिनयनमानन्दकोलाहलं

वन्दभ्भूतपिशाचनाथ वटुकं क्षभ्भस्य पालं शिवम् ॥

२) रुरुभैरव ध्यानम् ।

निर्वाणं निर्विकल्पं निरूपजमलं निर्विकारं क्षकारं

हुङ्कारं वज्रदंष्ट्रं हुतवहनयनं रौद्रमुन्मत्तभावम् ।

भट्कारं भक्तनागं भृकुटितमुखं भैरवं शूलपाणिं

वन्दभ्खड्गं कपालं डमरुकसहितं क्षभ्भापालन्नमामि ॥

३) चण्डभैरव ध्यानम् ।

बिभ्राणं शुभ्रवर्णं द्विगुणदशभुजं पञ्चवक्त्रन्त्रिनभ्भ

दानञ्छत्रभ्भुहस्तं रजतहिममृतं शङ्खभभ्भस्यचापम् ।

शूलं खड्गञ्च बाणं डमरुकसिकतावञ्चिमालोक्य मालां

सर्वाभीतिञ्च दोर्भीं भुजतगिरियुतं भैरवं सर्वसिद्धिम् ॥

४) क्रोधभैरव ध्यानम् ।

उद्यद्भास्कररूपनिभन्त्रिनयनं रक्ताङ्ग रागाम्बुजं
    भस्माद्यां वरदं कपालमभयं शूलन्दधानं करभ्र
नीलग्रीवमुदारभूषणशतं शन्तश्रु मूढोज्ज्वलं
    बन्धूकारुण वास अस्तमभयं दक्षं सदा भावयन्म ॥

५) उन्मत्तभैरव ध्यानम् ।

एकं खट्वाङ्गहस्तं पुनरपि भुजगं पाशमश्रन्त्रिशूलं
    कपालं खड्गहस्तं डमरुकसहितं वामहस्तश्रपिनाकम् ।
चन्द्रार्कं क्षशुमालां विकृतिसुकृतिनं सर्वयज्ञोपवीतं
    कालं कालान्तकारं मम भयहरं क्षश्रपालन्नमामि ॥

६) कपालभैरव ध्यानम् ।

वन्दश्रालं स्फटिकसदृशं कुम्भलोल्लासिवक्त्रं
    दिव्याकल्पैफणिमणिमयैकिङ्किणीनूपुरञ्च ।
दिव्याकारं विशदवदनं सुप्रसन्नं द्विनश्रं
    हस्ताद्यां वा दधानान्त्रिशिवमनिभयं वक्रदण्डौ कपालम् ॥

७) भीषणभैरव ध्यानम् ।

त्रिनश्र रक्तवर्णञ्च सर्वाभरणभूषितम् ।
कपालं शूलहस्तञ्च वरदाभयपाणिनम् ॥
सव्यश्रूलधरं भीमं खट्वाङ्गं वामकश्रावम् ।
रक्तवस्त्रपरिधानं रक्तमाल्यानुलश्रनम् ।
नीलग्रीवञ्च सौम्यञ्च सर्वाभरणभूषितम् ॥
नीलमश्र समाख्यातं कूर्चकश्रान्त्रिनश्रकम् ।
नागभूषञ्च रौद्रञ्च शिरोमालाविभूषितम् ॥
नूपुरस्वनपादञ्च सर्प यज्ञोपवीतिनम् ।
किङ्किणीमालिका भूष्यं भीमरूपं भयावहम् ॥

८) संहारभैरव ध्यानम् ।

एकवक्त्रन्त्रिनभ्रुञ्च हस्तयो द्वादशन्तथा ।
डमरुञ्चाङ्कुशं बाणं खड्गं शूलं भयान्वितम् ॥

धनुर्बाण कपालञ्च गदाग्निं वरदन्तथा ।
वामसव्यभ्रु पार्श्वेन आयुधानां विधन्तथा ॥

नीलमभ्रस्वरूपन्तु नीलवस्त्रोत्तरीयकम् ।
कस्तूर्यादि निलभ्रुञ्च श्वभ्रगन्धाक्षतन्तथा ॥

श्वभ्रार्क पुष्पमालाञ्च त्रिकोट्यङ्गणसङ्क्रिताम् ।
सर्वालङ्कार संयुक्तां संहारञ्च प्रकीर्तितम् ॥

इति श्रीभैरव स्तुति निरुद्र कुरुतभ्र

इति अष्टभैरव ध्यानस्तोत्रं सम्पूर्णम् ।

*****

Śrī Bhairava Sarva Phalaprada Stotram
श्रीभैरवसर्वफलप्रदस्तोत्रम्

Sarva Phala – all results i.e. This verse when chant with full devotion will provide any desired result.

ॐ भं भैरवाय अनिष्टनिवारणाय स्वाहा ।

मम सर्वे ग्रहाः अनिष्टनिवारणाय स्वाहा ।

ज्ञानं देहि धनं देहि मम द्रारिद्रयदुःखनिवारणाय स्वाहा ।

सुतं देहि यशो देहि मम गृहक्लेशनिवारणाय स्वाहा ।

स्वास्थ्य देहि बलं देहि मम शत्रुनिवारणाय स्वाहा ।

सिद्धिं देहि जयं देहि मम सर्वऋणनिवारणाय स्वाहा ।

ॐ भं भैरवाय अनिष्टनिवारणाय स्वाहा ।

इति श्रीभैरवसर्वफलप्रदस्तोत्रं सम्पूर्णम् ।

Oṃ Bhaṃ Bhairavāya Aniṣṭanivāraṇāya Svāhā |
Mama Sarve Grahāḥ Aniṣṭanivāraṇāya Svāhā |
Jñānaṃ Dehi Dhanaṃ Dehi Mama Drāridrayaduḥkhanivāraṇāya Svāhā |
Sutaṃ Dehi Yaśo Dehi Mama Gṛhakleśanivāraṇāya Svāhā |
Svāsthya Dehi Balaṃ Dehi Mama Śatrunivāraṇāya Svāhā |
Siddhiṃ Dehi Jayaṃ Dehi Mama Sarvaṝṇanivāraṇāya Svāhā |
Oṃ Bhaṃ Bhairavāya Aniṣṭanivāraṇāya Svāhā |

Iti Śrī Bhairava Sarvaphalaprada Stotraṃ Sampūrṇam |

*****

Śrī Bhairava Aṣṭakam

श्रीभैरवाष्टकम्

This is one of the important stotrams written by Sri Adi Shankara, who is an incarnation of Lord Shiva himself.

श्रीभैरवाय नमः ॥

दक्षराजसक्षमानपावनांघ्रिपङ्कजं
व्यालयज्ञसूत्रमिन्दुशक्षरं कृपाकरम् ।
नारदादियोगिवृन्दवन्दितं दिगंबरं
काशिकापुराधिनाथकालभैरवं भजभ्र ॥ १

भानुकोटिभास्वरं भवाब्धितारकं परं
नीलकण्ठमीप्सितार्थदायकं त्रिलोचनम् ।
कालकालमंबुजाक्षमक्षशूलमक्षरं
काशिकापुराधिनाथकालभैरवं भजभ्र ॥ २

शूलटंकपाशदण्डपाणिमादिकारणं
श्यामकायमादिदक्षमक्षरं निरामयम् ।
भीमविक्रमं प्रभुं विचित्रताण्डवप्रियं
काशिकापुराधिनाथकालभैरवं भजभ्र ॥ ३

भुक्तिमुक्तिदायकं प्रशस्तचारुविग्रहं
भक्तवत्सलं स्थितं समस्तलोकविग्रहम् ।
विनिक्वणन्मनोज्ञहेमकिङ्किणीलसत्कटिं
काशिकापुराधिनाथकालभैरवं भजभ्र ॥ ४

धर्मसेतुपालकं त्वधर्ममार्गनाशकं
कर्मपाशमोचकं सुशर्मदायकं विभुम् ।
स्वर्णवर्णशेषपाशशोभितांगमण्डलं
काशिकापुराधिनाथकालभैरवं भजभ्र ॥ ५

रत्नपादुकाप्रभाभिरामपादयुग्मकं
नित्यमद्वितीयमिष्टदैवतं निरंजनम् ।
मृत्युदर्पनाशनं करालदंष्ट्रमोक्षदं
काशिकापुराधिनाथकालभैरवं भजश्र ६

अट्टहासभिन्नपद्मजाण्डकोशसंततिं
दृष्टिपातनष्टपापजालमुग्रशासनम् ।
अष्टसिद्धिदायकं कपालमालिकाधरं
काशिकापुराधिनाथकालभैरवं भजश्र ७

भूतसंघनायकं विशालकीर्तिदायकं
काशिवासलोकपुण्यपापशोधकं विभुम् ।
नीतिमार्गकोविदं पुरातनं जगत्पतिं
काशिकापुराधिनाथकालभैरवं भजश्र ८

फल श्रुति ॥

कालभैरवाष्टकं पठंति यश्रमनोहरं
ज्ञानमुक्तिसाधनं विचित्रपुण्यवर्धनम् ।
शोकमोहदैन्यलोभकोपतापनाशनं
प्रयान्ति कालभैरवांघ्रिसन्निधिं नरा ध्रुवम् ॥

॥ इति श्रीमत्परमहंसपरिव्राजकाचर्यस्य श्रीगोविन्दभगवत्पूज्यपादशिष्यस्य
श्रीमच्छङ्करभगवतः कृतौ श्री कालभैरवाष्टकं सम्पूर्णम् ॥

Śrībhairavāṣṭakam

Śrī Bhairavāya Namaḥ ॥

Devarājasevyamānapāvanāmghripaṅkajaṃ
Vyālayajñasūtraminduśekharaṃ Kṛpākaram |
Nāradādiyogivṛndavanditaṃ Digambaraṃ
Kāśikāpurādhināthakālabhairavaṃ Bhaje ॥   1

Bhānukoṭibhāsvaraṃ Bhavābdhitārakaṃ Paraṃ
Nīlakaṇṭhamīpsitārthadāyakaṃ Trilocanam |
Kālakālamambujākṣamakṣaśūlamakṣaraṃ
Kāśikāpurādhināthakālabhairavaṃ Bhaje || 2

Śūlaṭaṃkapāśadaṇḍapāṇimādikāraṇaṃ
Śyāmakāyamādidevamakṣaraṃ Nirāmayam |
Bhīmavikramaṃ Prabhuṃ Vicitratāṇḍavapriyaṃ
Kāśikāpurādhināthakālabhairavaṃ Bhaje || 3

Bhuktimuktidāyakaṃ Praśastacāruvigrahaṃ
Bhaktavatsalaṃ Sthitaṃ Samastalokavigraham |
Vinikvaṇanmanojñahemakiṅkiṇīlasatkaṭiṃ
Kāśikāpurādhināthakālabhairavaṃ Bhaje || 4

Dharmasetupālakaṃ Tvadharmamārganāśakaṃ
Karmapāśamocakaṃ Suśarmadāyakaṃ Vibhum |
Svarṇavarṇaśeṣapāśaśobhitāṃgamaṇḍalaṃ
Kāśikāpurādhināthakālabhairavaṃ Bhaje || 5

Ratnapādukāprabhābhirāmapādayugmakaṃ
Nityamadvitīyamiṣṭadaivataṃ Niraṃjanam |
Mṛtyudarpanāśanaṃ Karāladaṃṣṭramokṣadaṃ
Kāśikāpurādhināthakālabhairavaṃ Bhaje || 6

Aṭṭahāsabhinnapadmajāṇḍakośasaṃtatiṃ
Dṛṣṭipātanaṣṭapāpajālamugraśāsanam |
Aṣṭasiddhidāyakaṃ Kapālamālikādharaṃ
Kāśikāpurādhināthakālabhairavaṃ Bhaje || 7

Bhūtasaṃghanāyakaṃ Viśālakīrtidāyakaṃ
Kāśivāsalokapuṇyapāpaśodhakaṃ Vibhum |
Nītimārgakovidaṃ Purātanaṃ Jagatpatiṃ
Kāśikāpurādhināthakālabhairavaṃ Bhaje || 8

Phala Śruti ‖

Kālabhairavāṣṭakaṃ Paṭhaṃti Ye Manoharaṃ
Jñānamuktisādhanaṃ Vicitrapuṇyavardhanam |
Śokamohadainyalobhakopatāpanāśanaṃ Var Lobhadainya
Prayānti Kālabhairavāṃghrisannidhiṃ Narā Dhruvam ‖

Iti Śrīmatparamahaṃsaparivrājakācaryasya
Śrīgovindabhagavatpūjyapādaśiṣyasya
Śrīmacchaṅkarabhagavataḥ Kṛtau

Śrī Kālabhairavāṣṭakaṃ Sampūrṇam ‖

*****

64 *Bhairava Lords*

It has been mentioned in a text called 'Shivaparakrama' that Lord Shiva has 64 different forms. Corresponding to each of those 64 Lord forms of Shiva has a series of 64 Bhairavs. Each of those 64 Bharavas has consorts called Bhairavis. Below are the names of the 64 Shivamurtis, Bhairavs and Bhairavis.

64 Shivamurtis (Forms of Lord Shiva)		
1.	Linga Murthy	God Shiva's shapeless form
2.	Lingodhbhava Murthy	God Shiva emerging from shapeless form
3.	Mukhalingam	Lord Shiva with five faces
4.	Sadashiva Murthy	The secondary form of Lord Shiva with five faces
5.	Mahasadashiva Murthy	Lord Shiva with twenty-five faces
6.	Umamaheshvara Murthy	Lord Shiva with Goddess Uma (Parvati)
7.	Sukasana Murthy	Lord Shiva with his consort Goddess Uma in a pleasant mood
8.	Umesha Murthy	Lord Shiva with his consort Goddess Uma and in a Varadana pose
9.	Somaskandha Murthi	Lord Shiva with his consort Goddess Uma and Lord Skanda
10.	Vrishabhantika Murthy	Lord Shiva with his mount Nandi bull
11.	Chandrashekara Murthy	Lord Shiva with Moon in crescent form
12.	Bhujanga Lalita Murthy	Lord Shiva with Moon and Snake
13.	Sada Nritta Murthy	Lord Shiva dancing in the form of Natraj
14.	Gangavisarjana Murthy	Lord Shiva releasing Devi Ganga from his head
15.	Ardhanareeshvara Murthy	Lord Shiva with his consort in Ardhanareeshwara form – half Lord Shiva and half Goddess Parvati

16.	Vrushabharoodar	Lord Shiva with sitting on Nandi Bull
17.	Bhujanga Trasa Murthy	Lord Shiva with a snake in one hand and fire in the other hand
18.	Chandathandava Murthy	Lord Shiva standing on a demon in a fierce form
19.	Tripurantaka Murthy	Lord Shiva with his consort Goddess Uma, riding a chariot driven by four horses
20.	Gajasura Samhara Murthy	Lord Shiva battling an elephant demon
21.	Sandhya Nrutta Murthy	Lord Shiva with his consort Goddess Uma, with a damaroo in his hand
22.	Gangadhara Murthy	Lord Shiva with the Devi Ganga falling into matted locks
23.	Kalyanasundhara Murthy	Lord Shiva getting married to Goddess Uma
24.	Jvarabhagna Murthy	Lord Shiva who annihilates fever
25.	Shardhula Hara Murthy	Lord Shiva sitting on a tiger skin
26.	Keshavartha Murthy	Shankaranarayana form of Lord Shiva Lord Shiva with damaroo in one hand and chakra in the other
27.	Chandisha Anugraha Murthy	Lord Shiva gifting the Kamdhenu Cow to a Sage
28.	Vinadhara Dakshina Murthy	Lord Shiva playing Veena musical instrument
29.	Lakulishvara Murthy	Lord Shiva holding damaroo and trishool
30.	Vaduka Murthy	Bhairava form of Lord Shiva holding a snake and a bowl
31.	Agorastra Murthy	Lord Shiva in an Aghori form
32.	Guru Murthy	Lord Shiva as a sage teaching other sage
33.	Jalandharavata Murthy	Lord Shiva killing KIng Jalandhara
34.	Ekapadha Murthy	Lord Shiva standing on one leg
35.	Gaurilila Samanvita Murthy	Lord Shiva with his consort Goddess Uma, Lord Ganesha and Lord Skanda

36.	Brahma Shirachetha Murthy	Lord Shiva cursing Lord Brahma saying that he will never be worshipped
37.	Varaha Samhara Murthy	Lord Shiva killing Vishnu in his Varaha avatar
38.	Shishyabhava Murthy	Lord Shiva and Devi Parvati with his devotees
39.	Pashupatha Murthy	Larger than life form of Lord Shiva
40.	Bhikshatana Murthy	God Shiva asking for alms
41.	Vyakyana Dakshina Murthy	Lord Shiva killing a demon to restore Dharma
42.	Kalanthakar	Lord Shiva came out of a fire to kill a demon
43.	Bhairav Murthy	Bhairava form – Lord Shiva with a dog
44.	Kshetrapaala Murthy	Lord Shiva's another form where he is again seen with a dog
45.	Dakshayagyahara Murthy	Lord Shiva destroying the yagna of Daksha
46.	Ashvaruda Murthy	Lord Shiva sitting on a horse
47.	Ekapada Trimurthy	Lord Shiva with one foot seen taking the forms of Lord Vishnu and Lord Brahma
48.	Gaurivaraprada Murthy	Lord Shiva with his consort Devi Gauri
49.	Vishapaharana Murthy	Lord Shiva is seen resting with Devi Parvati sitting beside him
50.	Kurma Samhara Murthy	Lord Shiva with Lord Vishnu in his Kurma avatar
51.	Prarthana Murthy	Lord Shiva with Devi Parvati in a very happy mood
52.	Kankala Murthy	Lord Shiva seen in a standing pose
53.	Simhaghna Murthy	Lord Shiva with three heads of lion and killing a demon
54.	Yoga Dakshina Murthy	Lord Shiva as a yogic
55.	Kama Dahana Murthy	Lord Shiva burning cupids of Kamadeva
56.	Apatuttarana Murthy	Lord Shiva in a hermit form

57.	Veerabhadra Murthy	Lord Shiva as a warrior form
58.	Kiratha Murthy	Lord Shiva with bow and arrow
59.	Gajantika Murthy	Lord Shiva with an elephant
60.	Tripada Trimurthi	Lord Shiva is standing on three legd with Lord Vishnu and Lord Brahma
61.	Chakradanasvarupa Murthy	Lord Shiva giving Sudarshana Chakra to Lord Vishnu
62.	Garudanthika Murthy	Lord Shiva being worshipped by other Gods
63.	Matsya Samhara Murthy	Lord Shiva destroying Vishnu in a fish form
64.	Rakthabhiksha Pradana Murthy	Lord Shiva is seen with Lord Vishnu with trident

Names of 64 *Bhairavas* with consorts. The consorts are called as *Bhairavis* [8] or *Yoginees*. There are some minor differences between different schools in the names.

#	*Bhairava*	*Bhairavi/ Yogini*
1.	Neelakanta Bhairava	Jaya
2.	Vishalaksha Bhairava	Vijaya
3.	Martanda Bhairava	Jayant
4.	Mundana Prabhu Bhairava	Aparaajitha
5.	Svascanda Bhairava	Divya Mohini
6.	Athi Santhushta Bhairava	Maha Mohini
7.	Kechara Bhairava	Siddha Mohini
8.	Samhara Bhairava * @	Ganeshvara Mohini
9.	Vishva Roopa Bhairava	Prethasini
10.	Nanaa Roopa Bhairava	Daakinee
11.	Parama Bhairava	Kali
12.	Dandha Karna Bhairava	Kaalaraatri
13.	Sita Paatra Bhairava	Nicaashari
14.	Cheerita Bhairava	Dannkarri
15.	Unmatta Bhairava *	Vethaalya
16.	Megha Natha Bhairava	Hoomkari
17.	Mano Vegha Bhairava	Urdhva Keshi

---

[8] 276th name in Sri Lalita Sahasranama is 'Bhairavee'

#	Bhairava	Bhairavi/ Yogini
18.	Kshetrapalaka Bhairava	Viroobakshi
19.	Viroobaksha Bhairava	Sushpaangee
20.	Karala Bhairava	Nara Bojini
21.	Nirbaya Bhairava	Patchaarri
22.	Pishitha Bhairava	Veerabatra
23.	Prekshata Bhairava	Dhoomraakshi
24.	Loka Bala Bhairava	Kalakapriya
25.	Gadhaadhara Bhairava	Ghora Raktaakshi
26.	Vajrahasta Bhairava	Vishwaroopi
27.	Mahaa Kaala Bhairava	Abhayankari
28.	Prakanda Bhairava	Veera Koumari
29.	Pralaya Bhairava	Chandikai
30.	Antaka Bhairava	Vaaraahi
31.	Bhoomi Gharbha Bhairava	Munda Dhaarani
32.	Bheeshana Bhairava *	Raakshasi
33.	Samhara Bhairava * @	Bhairavi
34.	Kulapala Bhairava	Tvaankshini
35.	Rundamaalaa Bhairava	Dhoomraangi
36.	Raktaanga Bhairava	Preta Vaahini
37.	Pingalekshana Bhairava	Katgini
38.	Apraroopa Bhairava	Dheergalam Bhoshyaa
39.	Tara Bhalana Bhairava	Malini
40.	Praja Bhalana Bhairava	Mantra Mohini
41.	Kula Bhairava	Kali
42.	Mantra Nayaka Bhairava	Chakrini
43.	Rudra Bhairava	Kankali
44.	Pitaamaha Bhairava	Bhuvaneshwari
45.	Vishnu Bhairava	Trotaki
46.	Vatukanaata Bhairava	Mahaamaari
47.	Kapala Bhairava *	Yamadhooti
48.	Bhoota Vetaala Bhairava	Kali
49.	Trinetra Bhairava	Kesini
50.	Tripuraantaka Bhairava	Marddhini
51.	Varadha Bhairava	Rogajange
52.	Parvata Vaahana Bhairava	Nirvaani
53.	Shashi Vaahana Bhairava	Vishaali

#	Bhairava	Bhairavi/ Yogini
54.	Kapala Bhooshana Bhairava	Khaarmukhi
55.	Sarvagna Bhairava	Dotyamima
56.	Sarva Deva Bhairava	Adhomukhya
57.	Eshaana Bhairava	Mundakra Dhaarini
58.	Sarva Bhoota Bhairava	Vyaakrinee
59.	Ghoranaata Bhairava	Dhoonkshini
60.	Bhayankara Bhairava	Preta Roopini
61.	Bhuddhi Mukti Phala Pradha Bhairava	Dhoor Jatyai
62.	Kaalaagni Bhairava	Ghoryaa
63.	Mahaa Roudhra Bhairava	Karaali
64.	Dakshinaa Pistita Bhairava	Vishalankyaa

* These 4 names are among *Ashtānga Bhairavas* also.

@ These 2 names are repeated.

Among these 64 lords –

1. First 8 are in golden colour, holding trident, pasam, scepter, and a knife in 4 hands, shine so beautifully.

2. Second 8 are in white colour, holding a garland of beeds, a goad, a book, a Veena instrument and a garland made of beeds called Suketam, in 4 hands, shine so beautifully.

3. Third 8 are in Blue colour, holding a fire-pot, a shakti weapon, a maze and a spear, in 4 hands, shine so beautifully.

4. Fourth 8 are in smoke colour, holding a sword, a shield, a knife and a parashu, in 4 hands, shine so beautifully.

5. Fifth 8 are in white colour, holding a spear, a shield, an armour and a pindi, in 4 hands, shine so beautifully.

6. Sixth 8 are in yellow colour, holding a spear, a shield, an armour and a pindi, in 4 hands, shine so beautifully.

7. Seventh 8 are in red colour, holding a spear, a shield, an armour and a pindi, in 4 hands, shine so beautifully.

8. Eighth 8 are in white colour, holding a spear, a shield, an armour and a pindi, in 4 hands, shine so beautifully.

*****

Śrī Bhairava Aṣṭotra Śata Nāmāvaliḥ
श्री भैरव अष्ठोत्र शतनामावलि:

Om Swarṇa Vijayāya Vidmahe Śūla Hastāya Dhīmahi

Tanno Bhairava Pracodayāt ||

ॐ भैरवाय नम:	*Om Bhairavāya Namaḥ*
ॐ भूतनाथाय नम:	*Om Bhūtanāthāya Namaḥ*
ॐ भूतात्मनभ्राम:	*Om Bhūtātmane Namaḥ*
ॐ भूतभावनाय नम:	*Om Bhūtabhāvanāya Namaḥ*
ॐ क्षेत्रज्ञाय नम:	*Om Kṣetrajnāya Namaḥ*
ॐ क्षेत्रपालाय नम:	*Om Kṣetrapālāya Namaḥ*
ॐ क्षेत्रदाय नम:	*Om Kṣetradāya Namaḥ*
ॐ क्षत्रियाय नम:	*Om Kṣatriyāya Namaḥ*
ॐ विराजभ्राम:	*Om Viraje Namaḥ*
ॐ श्मशान वासिनभ्राम: 10	*Om Śmaśāna Vāsine Namaḥ* 10
ॐ मांसाशिनभ्राम:	*Om Māmsāśine Namaḥ*
ॐ खर्वराशिनभ्राम:	*Om Kharvarāśine Namaḥ*
ॐ स्मरांतकाय नम:	*Om Smarāmtakāya Namaḥ*
ॐ रक्तपाय नम:	*Om Raktapāya Namaḥ*
ॐ पानपाय नम:	*Om Pānapāya Namaḥ*
ॐ सिद्धाय नम:	*Om Siddhāya Namaḥ*
ॐ सिद्धिदाय नम:	*Om Siddhidāya Namaḥ*
ॐ सिद्धिसेविताय नम:	*Om Siddhisevitāya Namaḥ*
ॐ कंकालाय नम:	*Om Kamkālāya Namaḥ*
ॐ कालशमनाय नम: 20	*Om Kālāśamanāya Namaḥ* 20
ॐ कलाकाष्ठाय नम:	*Om Kalākāṣṭhāya Namaḥ*

ॐ तनयश्राम:	Om Tanaye Namaḥ
ॐ कवयश्राम:	Om Kavaye Namaḥ
ॐ त्रिनश्राय नम:	Om Trinetrāya Namaḥ
ॐ बहुनश्राय नम:	Om Bahunetrāya Namaḥ
ॐ पिंगललोचनाय नम:	Om Pingalalocanāya Namaḥ
ॐ शूलपाणयश्राम:	Om Śūlapāṇaye Namaḥ
ॐ खड्गपाणयश्राम:	Om Khaḍgapāṇaye Namaḥ
ॐ कपालिनश्राम:	Om Kapāline Namaḥ
ॐ धूम्रलोचनाय नम: 30	Om Dhūmralocanāya Namaḥ 30
ॐ अभीरवश्राम:	Om Abhīrave Namaḥ
ॐ भैरवीनाथाय नम:	Om Bhairavīnāthāya Namaḥ
ॐ भूतपाय नम:	Om Bhūtapāya Namaḥ
ॐ योगिनीपतयश्राम:	Om Yoginīpataye Namaḥ
ॐ धनधाय नम:	Om Dhanadhāya Namaḥ
ॐ धनहारिणश्राम:	Om Dhanahāriṇe Namaḥ
ॐ धनवतश्राम:	Om Dhanavate Namaḥ
ॐ प्रीतिवर्धनाय नम:	Om Prītivardhanāya Namaḥ
ॐ नागहाराय नम:	Om Nāgahārāya Namaḥ
ॐ नागपाशाय नम: 40	Om Nāgapāśāya Namaḥ 40
ॐ व्योमकश्राय नम:	Om Vyomakeśāya Namaḥ
ॐ कपालभृतश्राम:	Om Kapālabhrute Namaḥ
ॐ कालाय नम:	Om Kālāya Namaḥ
ॐ कपालमालिनश्राम:	Om Kapālamāline Namaḥ
ॐ कमनीयाय नम:	Om Kamanīyāya Namaḥ
ॐ कलानिधयश्राम:	Om Kalānidhaye Namaḥ

ॐ त्रिलोचनाय नम:	Om Trilocanāya Namaḥ
ॐ ज्वलन्नेत्राय नम:	Om Jvalannetrāya Namaḥ
ॐ त्रिशिखिने नम:	Om Triśikhine Namaḥ
ॐ त्रिलोकष्याय नम: 50	Om Trilokaṣāya Namaḥ 50
ॐ त्रिनेत्रयतनयाय नम:	Om Trinetrayatanayāya Namaḥ
ॐ डिंभाय नमह्	Om Ḍimbhāya Namah
ॐ शांताय नम:	Om Śāntāya Namaḥ
ॐ शांतजनप्रियाय नम:	Om Śāntajanapriyāya Namaḥ
ॐ बटुकाय नम:	Om Batukāya Namaḥ
ॐ बहुवेश्याय नम:	Om Bahuveśāya Namaḥ
ॐ खट्वांगधारकाय नम:	Om Khatvāngadhārakāya Namaḥ
ॐ भूताध्यक्षाय नम:	Om Bhūtādhyakṣāya Namaḥ
ॐ पशुपतये नम:	Om Paśupataye Namaḥ
ॐ भिक्षुकाय नम: 60	Om Bhikṣukāya Namaḥ 60
ॐ परिचारकाय नम:	Om Paricārakāya Namaḥ
ॐ धूर्ताय नम:	Om Dhūrtāya Namaḥ
ॐ दिगम्बराय नम:	Om Digambarāya Namaḥ
ॐ शूराय नम:	Om Śūrāya Namaḥ
ॐ हरिणे नम:	Om Hariṇe Namaḥ
ॐ पांडुलोचनाय नम:	Om Pāndulocanāya Namaḥ
ॐ प्रशांताय नम:	Om Praśāntāya Namaḥ
ॐ शांतिदाय नम:	Om Śāmtidāya Namaḥ
ॐ सिद्धाय नम:	Om Siddhāya Namaḥ

ॐ शंकरप्रियबांधवाय नम: 70	Om Śankarapriyabāndhavāya Namaḥ 70
ॐ अष्टमूर्तयभ्रम:	Om Aṣṭamūrtaye Namaḥ
ॐ निधीशाय नम:	Om Nidhīśāya Namaḥ
ॐ ज्ञानचक्षुशभ्रम:	Om Jnānachakṣuśe Namaḥ
ॐ तपोमदाय नम:	Om Tapomadāya Namaḥ
ॐ अष्टाधाराय नम:	Om Aṣṭādhārāya Namaḥ
ॐ षढाधाराय नम:	Om Ṣaḍādhārāya Namaḥ
ॐ सर्पयुक्ताय नम:	Om Sarpayuktāya Namaḥ
ॐ शिखिसखाय नम:	Om Śikhisakhāya Namaḥ
ॐ भूधराय नम:	Om Bhūdharāya Namaḥ
ॐ भुधराधीशाय नम: 80	Om Bhudharādhīśāya Namaḥ 80
ॐ भूपतयभ्रम:	Om Bhūpataye Namaḥ
ॐ भूधरात्मजाय नम:	Om Bhūdharātmajāya Namaḥ
ॐ कंकालधारिनभ्रम:	Om Kankāladhārine Namaḥ
ॐ मुण्डिनभ्रम:	Om Muṇḍine Namaḥ
ॐ नागयज्ञोपवीतवत: नम:	Om Nāgayajnopavītavate Namaḥ
ॐ जृंभणाय नम:	Om Jrumbhaṇāya Namaḥ
ॐ मोहनाय नम:	Om Mohanāya Namaḥ
ॐ स्तम्भिनभ्रम:	Om Stambhine Namaḥ
ॐ मारणाय नम:	Om Māraṇāya Namaḥ
ॐ क्षोभनाय नम: 90	Om Kṣobhanāya Namaḥ 90

ॐ शुद्धनीलांजनप्रख्याय नम:	Om Śuddhanīlāmjanaprakhyāya Namaḥ
ॐ दैत्यघ्नभ्रम:	Om Daityaghne Namaḥ
ॐ मुंडभूषिताय नम:	Om Muṇḍabhūṣitāya Namaḥ
ॐ बलिभुजे नम:	Om Balibhuje Namaḥ
ॐ बलिभूतनाथाय नम:	Om Balibhutanāthāya Namaḥ
ॐ बालाय नम:	Om Bālāya Namaḥ
ॐ बालपराक्रमाय नम:	Om Bālaparākramāya Namaḥ
ॐ सर्वपत्तारणाय नम:	Om Sarvapattāraṇāya Namaḥ
ॐ दुर्गाय नम:	Om Durgāya Namaḥ
ॐ दुष्ट भूषिताय नम: 100	Om Duṣṭabhūṣitāya Namaḥ 100
ॐ कामिनभ्रम:	Om Kāmine Namaḥ
ॐ कलानिधयभ्रम:	Om Kalānidhaye Namaḥ
ॐ कांताय नम:	Om Kāntāya Namaḥ
ॐ कामिनीवश कृद्धशिन: नम:	Om Kāminīvaśa Kruddhaśine Namaḥ
ॐ सर्वसिद्धिप्रदाय नम:	Om Sarvasiddhipradāya Namaḥ
ॐ वैद्याय नम:	Om Vaidyāya Namaḥ
ॐ प्रभवभ्रम:	Om Prabhave Namaḥ
ॐ विष्णवभ्रम: 108	Om Viṣṇave Namaḥ 108

Iti Sri Bhairava Aṣṭotra Śata Nāmāvali Sampūrnam

*****

Śrī Bhairava Sahasra Nāmāvaliḥ
श्री भैरव सहस्रनामावलि:

Om Namo Bhagavate Kālāya Ghorāya Vajra Dhamśtrāya |
Śatru Nāśāya Sarva Bhūta Damanāya Hūm Phat Svāhā ||

ॐ ह्रीं बटुकाय नम:		Om Hrīm Baṭukāya Namaḥ.
ॐ ह्रीं कामदाय नम:		Om Hrīm Kāmadāya Namaḥ.
ॐ ह्रीं नाथप्रियाय नम:		Om Hrīm Nāthapriyāya Namaḥ.
ॐ ह्रीं प्रभाकराय नम:		Om Hrīm Prabhākarāya Namaḥ.
ॐ ह्रीं भैरवाय नम:		Om Hrīm Bhairavōya Namaḥ.
ॐ ह्रीं भीतिग्ने नम:		Om Hrīm Bhītignē Namaḥ.
ॐ ह्रीं दर्प्पाय नम:		Om Hrīm Darpāya Namaḥ.
ॐ ह्रीं कन्दर्पाय नम:		Om Hrīm Kandarpāya Namaḥ.
ॐ ह्रीं मीनकक्षनाय नम:		Om Hrīm Mīnakētanāya Namaḥ.
ॐ ह्रीं रुद्राय नम:	10	Om Hrīm Rudrāya Namaḥ. 10
ॐ ह्रीं भूतेशाय नम:		Om Hrīm Bhūtēśāya Namaḥ.
ॐ ह्रीं भूतनाथाय नम:		Om Hrīm Bhūtanāthāya Namaḥ.
ॐ ह्रीं प्रजापतय नम:		Om Hrīm Prajāpatayē Namaḥ.
ॐ ह्रीं दयालवभ्रम:		Om Hrīm Dayālavē Namaḥ.
ॐ ह्रीं क्रूराय नम:		Om Hrīm Krūrāya Namaḥ.
ॐ ह्रीं ईशानाय नम:		Om Hrīm Īśānāya Namaḥ.
ॐ ह्रीं जनीशाय नम:		Om Hrīm Janīśāya Namaḥ.
ॐ ह्रीं लोकवल्लभाय नम:		Om Hrīm Lōkavallabhāya Namaḥ.

ॐ ह्रीं देव्वाय नम:		Om Hrīm Dēvāya Namaḥ.
ॐ ह्रीं दैत्येश्वराय नम:	20	Om Hrīm Daityēśvarāya Namaḥ. 20
ॐ ह्रीं वीराय नम:		Om Hrīm Vīrāya Namaḥ.
ॐ ह्रीं वीरवन्ध्याय नम:		Om Hrīm Vīravandyāya Namaḥ
ॐ ह्रीं दिवाकराय नम:		Om Hrīm Divākarāya Namaḥ.
ॐ ह्रीं बलिप्रियाय नम:		Om Hrīm Balipriyāya Namaḥ.
ॐ ह्रीं सुरश्रेष्ठाय नम:		Om Hrīm Suraśrēṣṭhāya Namaḥ.
ॐ ह्रीं कनिष्ठाय नम:		Om Hrīm Kaniṣṭhāya Namaḥ.
ॐ ह्रीं कनिष्ठ शिशुवे नम:		Om Hrīm Kaniṣṭha Śiśuvē Namaḥ.
ॐ ह्रीं महाबलाय नम:		Om Hrīm Mahābalāya Namaḥ.
ॐ ह्रीं महातेजस नम:		Om Hrīm Mahātējasē Namaḥ.
ॐ ह्रीं वित्तजित नम:	30	Om Hrīm Vittajitē Namaḥ. 30
ॐ ह्रीं द्युतिवर्धनाय नम:		Om Hrīm Dyutivardhaṉāya Namaḥ.
ॐ ह्रीं तेजस्विन नम:		Om Hrīm Tējasviṉē Namaḥ.
ॐ ह्रीं वीर्यवतभ्राम:		Om Hrīm Vīryavāṉāya Namaḥ.
ॐ ह्रीं वृद्धाय नम:		Om Hrīm Vru'ddhāya Namaḥ.
ॐ ह्रीं विवृद्धाय नम:		Om Hrīm Vivru'ddhāya Namaḥ.
ॐ ह्रीं भूतनायकाय नम:		Om Hrīm Bhūta Nāyakāya Namaḥ.
ॐ ह्रीं बालाय नम:		Om Hrīm Bālāya Namaḥ.
ॐ ह्रीं कपालाय नम:		Om Hrīm Kapālāya Namaḥ.
ॐ ह्रीं कामाय नम:		Om Hrīm Kāmāya Namaḥ.
ॐ ह्रीं विकामाय नम:	40	Om Hrīm Vikāmāya Namaḥ. 40

ॐ ह्रीं कामर्दनाय नम: ।	Om Hrīm Kāmamardaṇāya Namaḥ.
ॐ ह्रीं कामिका रमणाय नम:।	Om Hrīm Kāmikā Ramaṇāya Namaḥ.
ॐ ह्रीं कालि नायकाय नम: ।	Om Hrīm Kāmī Nāyakāya Namaḥ.
ॐ ह्रीं कालिकाप्रियाय नम: ।	Om Hrīm Kālikāpriyāya Namaḥ
ॐ ह्रीं कालीशाय नम: ।	Om Hrīm Kālīśāya Namaḥ.
ॐ ह्रीं कालिका कान्ताय नम: ।	Om Hrīm Kāminī Kāntāya Namaḥ.
ॐ ह्रीं कालिका नन्दवर्धनाय नम:।	Om Hrīm Kālikā Nanda Vardhaṇāya Namaḥ.
ॐ ह्रीं कालिका हृदय ज्ञानाय नम:	Om Hrīm Kālikā Hru'daya Jñāṇāya Namaḥ.
ॐ ह्रीं कालिका तनयाय नम:	Om Hrīm Kālikā Tanayāya Namaḥ.
ॐ ह्रीं नयाय नम: । 50	Om Hrīm Nayāya Namaḥ. 50
ॐ ह्रीं खगेश्वराय नम: ।	Om Hrīm Khagēśāya Namaḥ.
ॐ ह्रीं खेच्वराय नम: ।	Om Hrīm Khēcarāya Namaḥ.
ॐ ह्रीं खेड्याय नम: ।	Om Hrīm Khēṭāya Namaḥ.
ॐ ह्रीं विशिष्टाय नम: ।	Om Hrīm Viśiṣṭāya Namaḥ.
ॐ ह्रीं खड्गकप्रियाय नम: ।	Om Hrīm Kē²ṭakapriyāya Namaḥ.
ॐ ह्रीं कुमाराय नम: ।	Om Hrīm Kumārāya Namaḥ.
ॐ ह्रीं क्रोधनाय नम: ।	Om Hrīm Krōdhanāya Namaḥ.
ॐ ह्रीं कालाप्रियाय नम: ।	Om Hrīm Kālāpriyāya Namaḥ.
ॐ ह्रीं पर्वतरक्षकाय नम: ।	Om Hrīm Parvatarakṣakāya Namaḥ.
ॐ ह्रीं गणेज्याय नम: । 60	Om Hrīm Gaṇējyāya Namaḥ. 60

ॐ ह्रीं गणपाय नम:		Om Hrīm Gaṇapāya Namaḥ.
ॐ ह्रीं गूढाय नम:		Om Hrīm Gūḍhāya Namaḥ.
ॐ ह्रीं गूढाशये नम:		Om Hrīm Gūḍāśayāya Namaḥ.
ॐ ह्रीं गणेश्वराय नम:		Om Hrīm Gaṇēśvarāya Namaḥ.
ॐ ह्रीं गणनाथाय नम:		Om Hrīm Gaṇanātā²ya Namaḥ.
ॐ ह्रीं गणश्रेष्ठाय नम:		Om Hrīm Gaṇaśrēṣṭā²ya Namaḥ.
ॐ ह्रीं गणमुख्याय नम:		Om Hrīm Gaṇamuk²yāya Namaḥ.
ॐ ह्रीं गणप्रियाय नम:		Om Hrīm Gaṇapriyāya Namaḥ.
ॐ ह्रीं घोरनाथाय नम:		Om Hrīm Ghōranātā²ya Namaḥ.
ॐ ह्रीं घनश्यामाय नम:	70	Om Hrīm Ghanaśyāmāya Namaḥ. 70
ॐ ह्रीं घनमूर्तये नम:		Om Hrīm Ghanamūrtayē Namaḥ.
ॐ ह्रीं घनांतकाय नम:		Om Hrīm Ghaṇāntakāya Namaḥ.
ॐ ह्रीं चम्पकाय नम:		Om Hrīm Campakāya Namaḥ.
ॐ ह्रीं चिरञ्जीवाय नम:		Om Hrīm Cirañjīvāya Namaḥ.
ॐ ह्रीं चारुवेषाय नम:		Om Hrīm Cāruvēṣaśāya Namaḥ.
ॐ ह्रीं चराचराय नम:		Om Hrīm Carācarāya Namaḥ.
ॐ ह्रीं चिन्त्याय नम:		Om Hrīm Cintyāya Namaḥ.
ॐ ह्रीं अचिन्त्य गुणाय नम:		Om Hrīm Acintyō Guṇāya Namaḥ.
ॐ ह्रीं धीमते नम:		Om Hrīm Dhīmatē Namaḥ.

ॐ ह्रीं सुचित्तस्थाय नमः	80	Om Hrīm Sucittasdāya Namaḥ.
ॐ ह्रीं क्षितीश्वराय नमः		Om Hrīm Citīśvarāya Namaḥ.
ॐ ह्रीं छत्रिनभ्राम:		Om Hrīm Chatriṇē Namaḥ.
ॐ ह्रीं छत्रपतये नमः		Om Hrīm Chatrapatayē Namaḥ.
ॐ ह्रीं छत्राय नमः		Om Hrīm Chatrāya Namaḥ.
ॐ ह्रीं छिन्ननासामन: प्रियाय नमः|	Om Hrīm Chinnanāsāmanaḥ Priyāya Namaḥ.
ॐ ह्रीं छिन्नाभाय नमः:		Om Hrīm Chinnābhāya Namaḥ.
ॐ ह्रीं छिन्नसन्तापाय नमः		Om Hrīm Chinnasantāpāya Namaḥ.
ॐ ह्रीं छर्दिराय नमः:		Om Hrīm Chardirāya Namaḥ.
ॐ ह्रीं छर्दिनन्दनाय नमः:		Om Hrīm Chardinandanāya Namaḥ.
ॐ ह्रीं जब्बाय नमः:	90	Om Hrīm Jētāya Namaḥ. 90
ॐ ह्रीं जनाय नमः:		Om Hrīm Janāya Namaḥ.
ॐ ह्रीं जिष्णवभ्राम:		Om Hrīm Jiṣṇuvē Namaḥ.
ॐ ह्रीं जटीशानाय नमः:		Om Hrīm Jaṭīśānāya Namaḥ.
ॐ ह्रीं जनभ्राय नमः:		Om Hrīm Janēśvarāya Namaḥ.
ॐ ह्रीं जनकाय नमः:		Om Hrīm Janakāya Namaḥ.
ॐ ह्रीं जनसन्तोषाय नमः:		Om Hrīm Janasantōṣāya Namaḥ.
ॐ ह्रीं जन जाड्य विनाशनाय नमः:		Om Hrīm Jana Jāḍya Vināśanāya Namaḥ.
ॐ ह्रीं जालन्द्राय नमः:		Om Hrīm Jālandrāya Namaḥ.

ॐ ह्रीं जनप्रस्थाय नम:		Om Hrīm Janaprasdāya Namaḥ.
ॐ ह्रीं जनाराध्याय नम: |100	Om Hrīm Janārādhyāya Namaḥ. 100
ॐ ह्रीं जनाध्यक्षाय नम:		Om Hrīm Janādhyakṣāya Namaḥ.
ॐ ह्रीं जनप्रियाय नम:		Om Hrīm Janapriyāya Namaḥ.
ॐ ह्रीं जीवग्न नम:		Om Hrīm Jīvagne Namaḥ.
ॐ ह्रीं जीवदाय नम:		Om Hrīm Jīvadāya Namaḥ.
ॐ ह्रीं जन्तवभ्राम:		Om Hrīm Jantavē Namaḥ.
ॐ ह्रीं जीवनाथाय नम:		Om Hrīm Jīvanāthāya Namaḥ.
ॐ ह्रीं जनश्वराय नम:		Om Hrīm Janēśvarāya Namaḥ.
ॐ ह्रीं जयदाय नम:		Om Hrīm Jayadāya Namaḥ.
ॐ ह्रीं जित्वराय नम:		Om Hrīm Jitvarāya Namaḥ.
ॐ ह्रीं जिष्णुवभ्राम:	110	Om Hrīm Jiṣṇuvē Namaḥ. 110
ॐ ह्रीं जयश्रीयाय नम:		Om Hrīm Jayaśrīyāya Namaḥ.
ॐ ह्रीं जयवर्धनाय नम:		Om Hrīm Jayavardhanāya Namaḥ.
ॐ ह्रीं जयाभूमयभ्राम:		Om Hrīm Jayābhūmayē Namaḥ.
ॐ ह्रीं जयाकाराय नम:		Om Hrīm Jayākārāya Namaḥ.
ॐ ह्रीं जयहभ्रुवभ्राम:		Om Hrīm Jayahētuvē Namaḥ.
ॐ ह्रीं जयश्वराय नम:		Om Hrīm Jayēśvarāya Namaḥ.
ॐ ह्रीं झङ्कारहृद नन्तात्मन नम:		Om Hrīm Jhaṅkārahru'da Nantātmanē Namaḥ.
ॐ ह्रीं झङ्कार हभ्रुवभ्राम:		Om Hrīm Jhaṅkāra Hētuvē Namaḥ.

ॐ ह्रीं आत्मभुव नम:		Om Hrīm Ātmabhuvē Namah.
ॐ ह्रीं जभैश्वराय नम:	120	Om Hrīm Jabhaiśvarāya Namah. 120
ॐ ह्रीं हरयभ्राम:		Om Hrīm Harayē Namah.
ॐ ह्रीं भर्त्रे नम:		Om Hrīm Bhartrē Namah.
ॐ ह्रीं विभर्त्रे नम:		Om Hrīm Vibhartrē Namah.
ॐ ह्रीं भृत्यकश्वराय नम:		Om Hrīm Bhru'tyakēśvarāya Namah.
ॐ ह्रीं ठीकारहृदयाय नम:		Om Hrīm Ṭhīkārahru'dayāya Namah.
ॐ ह्रीं आत्मन नम:		Om Hrīm Ātmaṉē Namah.
ॐ ह्रीं ठङ्कश्राय नम:		Om Hrīm Ṭhaṅkēśāya Namah.
ॐ ह्रीं ठङ्कनायकाय नम:		Om Hrīm Ṭhaṅkanāyakāya Namah.

ॐ ह्रीं ठकारभुवब्भ्राम:		Om Hrīm Ṭhakārabhuvē Namaḥ.
ॐ ह्रीं अष्टरन्ध्रश्नाय नम:	130	Om Hrīm Aṣṭharandhrēśāya Namaḥ. 130
ॐ ह्रीं अष्टिरीशाय नम:		Om Hrīm Aṣṭhirīśāya Namaḥ.
ॐ ह्रीं ठकुरपतय नम:		Om Hrīm Ṭhakurapatayē Namaḥ.
ॐ ह्रीं डुंडिनभ्राम:		Om Hrīm Ḍuṇḍinē Namaḥ.
ॐ ह्रीं डक्का प्रियाय नम:		Om Hrīm Ḍakkā priyāya Namaḥ.
ॐ ह्रीं पान्थाय नम:		Om Hrīm Pānthāya Namaḥ.
ॐ ह्रीं डुण्ढिराजाय नम:		Om Hrīm Ḍuṇḍhirājāya Namaḥ.
ॐ ह्रीं निरन्तकाय नम:		Om Hrīm Nirantakāya Namaḥ.
ॐ ह्रीं ताम्राय नम:		Om Hrīm Tāmrāya Namaḥ.
ॐ ह्रीं तमीश्वराय नम:		Om Hrīm Stamīśvarāya Namaḥ.
ॐ ह्रीं स्रोतायाय नम:	140	Om Hrīm Strōtāyāya Namaḥ.
ॐ ह्रीं तीर्थराजाय नम:		Om Hrīm Thīrtarājāya Namaḥ.
ॐ ह्रीं तडित्प्रभव नम:		Om Hrīm Taḍitprabhavē Namaḥ.
ॐ ह्रीं त्रयक्षकाय नम:		Om Hrīm Trayakṣakāya Namaḥ.
ॐ ह्रीं ऋक्षराय नम:		Om Hrīm Ru'kṣarāya Namaḥ.
ॐ ह्रीं स्तभाय नम:		Om Hrīm Stabhāya Namaḥ.
ॐ ह्रीं स्तार्क्ष्यकाय नम:		Om Hrīm Ṭtārkṣyakāya Namaḥ.
ॐ ह्रीं स्ताक्षकाय नम:		Om Hrīm Stākṣakāya Namaḥ.
ॐ ह्रीं स्तम्भदश्वराय नम:		Om Hrīm Stambhadēśvarāya Namaḥ.

ॐ ह्रीं स्थलजाय नमः		Om Hrīm Sthalajāya Namaḥ.
ॐ ह्रीं स्थावराय नमः	150	Om Hrīm Sthāvarāya Namaḥ.
ॐ ह्रीं स्थात्रे नमः		Om Hrīm Sthātrē Namaḥ.
ॐ ह्रीं स्थिरबुद्धय नमः		Om Hrīm Sthirabuddhayē Namaḥ.
ॐ ह्रीं स्थितेन्द्रियाय नमः		Om Hrīm Sthitēndriyāya Namaḥ.
ॐ ह्रीं स्थिरज्ञाताय नमः		Om Hrīm Sthirajñātāya Namaḥ.
ॐ ह्रीं स्थिरप्रीतय नमः		Om Hrīm Sthiraprītayē Namaḥ.
ॐ ह्रीं स्थिराय नमः		Om Hrīm Sthirāya Namaḥ.
ॐ ह्रीं स्थिताय नमः		Om Hrīm Sthitāya Namaḥ.
ॐ ह्रीं स्थिराशयभ्राम		Om Hrīm Sthirāśayē Namaḥ.
ॐ ह्रीं दराय नमः		Om Hrīm Darāya Namaḥ.
ॐ ह्रीं दामोदराय नमः	160	Om Hrīm Dāmōdarāya Namaḥ.
ॐ ह्रीं दम्भाय नमः		Om Hrīm Dambhāya Namaḥ.
ॐ ह्रीं दाडिमी कुसुमप्रियाय नमः		Om Hrīm Dāḍimī Kusuma Priyāya Namaḥ.
ॐ ह्रीं दरिद्रग्नभ्राम		Om Hrīm Darifragṉē Namaḥ.
ॐ ह्रीं दमिनभ्राम		Om Hrīm Damiṉē Namaḥ.
ॐ ह्रीं दिव्याय नमः		Om Hrīm Divyāya Namaḥ.
ॐ ह्रीं दिव्यदह्णाय नमः		Om Hrīm Divyadēhāya Namaḥ.
ॐ ह्रीं दिवप्रभवभ्राम		Om Hrīm Divaprabhavē Namaḥ.
ॐ ह्रीं दिनकराय नमः		Om Hrīm Diṉakarāya Namaḥ.

ॐ ह्रीं दीक्षाकाराय नम:		Om Hrīm Dīkṣākārāya Namaḥ.
ॐ ह्रीं दिवानाथाय नम:	170	Om Hrīm Divānāthāya Namaḥ. 170
ॐ ह्रीं दिवसेश्राय नम:		Om Hrīm Divasēśāya Namaḥ.
ॐ ह्रीं दिवाकराय नम:		Om Hrīm Divākarāya Namaḥ.
ॐ ह्रीं दीर्घचराय नम:		Om Hrīm Dīrghacarāya Namaḥ.
ॐ ह्रीं दल ज्योतिषभ्राम:		Om Hrīm Dalajyōtiśē Namaḥ.
ॐ ह्रीं दलेश्राय नम:		Om Hrīm Dalēśāya Namaḥ.
ॐ ह्रीं दलसुन्दराय नम:		Om Hrīm Dalasundarāya Namaḥ.
ॐ ह्रीं दलप्रियाय नम:		Om Hrīm Dalapriyāya Namaḥ.
ॐ ह्रीं दलाभाशाय नम:		Om Hrīm Dalābhāśāya Namaḥ.
ॐ ह्रीं दलश्रेष्ठाय नम:		Om Hrīm Dalaśrēṣṭhāya Namaḥ.
ॐ ह्रीं दलप्रभवभ्राम:	180	Om Hrīm Dala prabhavē Namaḥ. 180
ॐ ह्रीं दलकान्तये नम:		Om Hrīm Dalakāntayē Namaḥ.
ॐ ह्रीं दलाकाराय नम:		Om Hrīm Dalākārāya Namaḥ.
ॐ ह्रीं दलसेव्याय नम:		Om Hrīm Dalasēvyāya Namaḥ.
ॐ ह्रीं दलार्चिताय नम:		Om Hrīm Dalārcitāya Namaḥ.
ॐ ह्रीं दीर्घबाहवभ्राम:		Om Hrīm Dīrghabāhavē Namaḥ.
ॐ ह्रीं दलश्रेष्ठाय नम:		Om Hrīm Dala Śrēṣṭhāya Namaḥ.

ॐ ह्रीं दललुप्ताय नम:		Om Hrīm Dalaluptāya Namah.
ॐ ह्रीं दलाकृतय नम:		Om Hrīm Dalākru'tayē Namah.
ॐ ह्रीं दानवस्याय नम:		Om Hrīm Dānavasyāya Namah.
ॐ ह्रीं दानवेश्राय नम:	190	Om Hrīm Dānavēśāya Namah.
ॐ ह्रीं दयासिन्धुवश्राम:		Om Hrīm Dayāsindhuvē Namah.
ॐ ह्रीं दयालवश्राम:		Om Hrīm Dayālavē Namah.
ॐ ह्रीं दीनवल्लभाय नम:		Om Hrīm Dīnavallabhāya Namah.
ॐ ह्रीं धनश्राय नम:		Om Hrīm Danēśāya Namah.
ॐ ह्रीं धनदाय नम:		Om Hrīm Danadāya Namah.
ॐ ह्रीं धर्माय नम:		Om Hrīm Darmāya Namah.
ॐ ह्रीं धनराजाय नम:		Om Hrīm Dhanarājāya Namah.
ॐ ह्रीं धनप्रभव नम:		Om Hrīm Dhanaprabhavē Namah.
ॐ ह्रीं धनप्रियाय नम:		Om Hrīm Dhanapriyāya Namah.
ॐ ह्रीं धनप्रदाय नम:	200	Om Hrīm Dhanapradāya Namah.

ॐ ह्रीं धनाध्यक्षाय नम:		Om Hrīm Dhanādhyakṣāya Bhamah.
ॐ ह्रीं धनमान्याय नम:		Om Hrīm Dhanamān'yāya Namah.
ॐ ह्रीं धनञ्जयाय नम:		Om Hrīm Dhanañjayāya Namah.
ॐ ह्रीं धीवराय नम:		Om Hrīm Dhīvarāya Namah.
ॐ ह्रीं धातुकाय नम:		Om Hrīm Dhātukāya Namah.

ॐ ह्रीं धात्र नम:		Om Hrīm Dhātrē Namaḥ.
ॐ ह्रीं धृवाय नम:		Om Hrīm Dhruvāya Namaḥ.
ॐ ह्रीं धूम्राय नम:		Om Hrīm Dhūmrāya Namaḥ.
ॐ ह्रीं धूमच्छवभ्राम:		Om Hrīm Dhūmacchavē Namaḥ.
ॐ ह्रीं धूमच्छविवर्धनाय नम:	210	Om Hrīm Dhūmaccha Vivardhanāya Namaḥ. 210
ॐ ह्रीं धनाय नम:		Om Hrīm Dhanāyaya Namaḥ.
ॐ ह्रीं धनिष्ठाय नम:		Om Hrīm Dhaniṣṭhāya Namaḥ.
ॐ ह्रीं धनलच्छराय नम:		Om Hrīm Dhanalacchatrāya Namaḥ.
ॐ ह्रीं धनकाम्याय नम:		Om Hrīm Dhanakāmyāya Namaḥ.
ॐ ह्रीं धनश्वराय नम:		Om Hrīm Dhanēśvarāya Namaḥ.
ॐ ह्रीं धीराय नम:		Om Hrīm Dhīrāya Namaḥ.
ॐ ह्रीं धीरतराय नम:		Om Hrīm Dhīratarāya Namaḥ.
ॐ ह्रीं धन्रुवभ्राम:		Om Hrīm Dhēnuvē Namaḥ.
ॐ ह्रीं ध्रिरिश्शाय नम:		Om Hrīm Dhīrēśāya Namaḥ.
ॐ ह्रीं धरणीप्रभुव नम:	220	Om Hrīm Dharaṇīprabhuvē Namaḥ. 220
ॐ ह्रीं धरानाथाय नम:		Om Hrīm Dharānāthāya Namaḥ.
ॐ ह्रीं धराधीशाय नम:		Om Hrīm Dhāranāthāya Namaḥ.
ॐ ह्रीं धात्रनाथाय नम:		Om Hrīm Dharādhīśāya Namaḥ.
ॐ ह्रीं धरणीनायकाय नम:		Om Hrīm Dharaṇīnāyakāya Namaḥ.
ॐ ह्रीं धराय नम:		Om Hrīm Dharāya Namaḥ.
ॐ ह्रीं धराकान्ताय नम:		Om Hrīm Dharākāntāya Namaḥ.

ॐ ह्रीं धरापालाय नम:		Om Hrīm Dharāpālāya Namaḥ.
ॐ ह्रीं धरणी जन वल्लभाय नम:		Om Hrīm Dharaṇī Jana Vallabhāya Namaḥ.
ॐ ह्रीं धराधाराय नम:		Om Hrīm Dharādharāya Namaḥ.
ॐ ह्रीं धराय नम:	230	Om Hrīm Dharāya Namaḥ. 230
ॐ ह्रीं धृष्णाय नम:		Om Hrīm Dhru'ṣṇāya Namaḥ.

ॐ ह्रीं धृतराष्ट्राय नम:		Om Hrīm Dhru'tarāṣṭrāya Namaḥ.
ॐ ह्रीं धनीश्वराय नम:		Om Hrīm Dhanīśvarāya Namaḥ.
ॐ ह्रीं नारदाय नम:		Om Hrīm Nāradāya Namaḥ.
ॐ ह्रीं नरदाय नम:		Om Hrīm Naradāya Namaḥ.
ॐ ह्रीं नेत्राय नम:		Om Hrīm Nētāya Namaḥ.
ॐ ह्रीं नीतिपूज्याय नम:		Om Hrīm Nītipūjyāya Namaḥ.
ॐ ह्रीं नतिपूज्याय नम:		Om Hrīm Natipūjyāya Namaḥ.
ॐ ह्रीं नतिप्रभुव नम:		Om Hrīm Natiprabhūvē Namaḥ.
ॐ ह्रीं नीतिलभ्याय नम:	240	Om Hrīm Nītilabhyāya Namaḥ.
ॐ ह्रीं नतीशनाय नम:		Om Hrīm Natīśāṉāya Namaḥ.
ॐ ह्रीं नतिलब्धाय नम:		Om Hrīm Natilabtāya Namaḥ.
ॐ ह्रीं नतीश्वराय नम:		Om Hrīm Natīśvarāya Namaḥ.
ॐ ह्रीं पार्थिवाय नम:		Om Hrīm Pārthivāya Namaḥ.
ॐ ह्रीं पाण्डवाय नम:		Om Hrīm Pāṇḍavāya Namaḥ.
ॐ ह्रीं पार्थ सम्पूज्याय नम:		Om Hrīm Pārtha Sampūjyāya Namaḥ.
ॐ ह्रीं पार्थोदाय नम:		Om Hrīm Pārthōdāya Namaḥ.
ॐ ह्रीं प्राणदाय नम:		Om Hrīm Prāṇadāya Namaḥ.
ॐ ह्रीं पार्थ प्राणदाय नम:		Om Hrīm Pārtha Prāṇadāya Namaḥ.
ॐ ह्रीं पृथुव नम:	250	Om Hrīm Pru'thuvē Namaḥ.
ॐ ह्रीं पुराणाय नम:		Om Hrīm Purāṇāya Namaḥ.
ॐ ह्रीं प्राणदाय नम:		Om Hrīm Prāṇadāya Namaḥ.

ॐ ह्रीं पान्थाय नम:		Om Hrīm Pānthāya Namaḥ.
ॐ ह्रीं पाञ्चालाय नम:		Om Hrīm Pāñcālāya Namaḥ.
ॐ ह्रीं पावकाय नम:		Om Hrīm Pāvakāya Namaḥ.
ॐ ह्रीं प्रभवभ्राम:		Om Hrīm Prabhavē Namaḥ.
ॐ ह्रीं पृथिवीशाय नम:		Om Hrīm Pru'thivīśāya Namaḥ.
ॐ ह्रीं पृथासूनवभ्राम:		Om Hrīm Pru'thāsūnavē Namaḥ.
ॐ ह्रीं पृथिवी भृत्यकक्षराय नम:		Om Hrīm Pru'thivī Pru'tyakēśvarāya Namaḥ.
ॐ ह्रीं पूर्वाय नम:	260	Om Hrīm Pūrvāya Namaḥ. 260
ॐ ह्रीं शूरपतय नम:		Om Hrīm Rūrapatayē Namaḥ.
ॐ ह्रीं श्रप्रसे नम:		Om Hrīm Rērēyasē Namaḥ.
ॐ ह्रीं प्रीतिदाय नम:		Om Hrīm Prītidāya Namaḥ.
ॐ ह्रीं प्रीतिवर्धनाय नम:		Om Hrīm Prītivartanāya Namaḥ.
ॐ ह्रीं पार्वतीशाय नम:		Om Hrīm Pārvatīśāya Namaḥ.
ॐ ह्रीं परक्ष्ञानाय नम:		Om Hrīm Parēśanāya Namaḥ.
ॐ ह्रीं पार्वती हृदय प्रियाय नम:		Om Hrīm Pārvatī Hru'daya Priyāya Namaḥ.
ॐ ह्रीं पार्वती रमणाय नम:		Om Hrīm Pārvatī Ramaṇāya Namaḥ.
ॐ ह्रीं पूताय नम:		Om Hrīm Pūtāya Namaḥ.
ॐ ह्रीं पवित्राय नम:	270	Om Hrīm Pavitrāya Namaḥ.
ॐ ह्रीं पापनाशनाय नम:		Om Hrīm Pāpanāśanāya Namaḥ.
ॐ ह्रीं पात्रिणभ्राम:		Om Hrīm Pātriṇē Namaḥ.
ॐ ह्रीं पात्रालि सन्तुष्ठाय नम:		Om Hrīm Pātrāli Santuṣṭāya Namaḥ.
ॐ ह्रीं परितुष्ठाय नम:		Om Hrīm Parituṣṭāya Namaḥ.

ॐ ह्रीं पुमाम्साय नम: |	Om Hrīm Pumāmsāya Namaḥ.
ॐ ह्रीं प्रियाय नम: |	Om Hrīm Priyāya Namaḥ.
ॐ ह्रीं पर्वेशाय नम: |	Om Hrīm Parvēśāya Namaḥ.
ॐ ह्रीं पर्वता धीशाय नम: |	Om Hrīm Parvata Dhīśāya Namaḥ.
ॐ ह्रीं पर्वतो नायकात्मजाय नम:|	Om Hrīm Parvatō Nāyakātmajāya Namaḥ.
ॐ ह्रीं फाल्गुनाय नम: | 280	Om Hrīm Pālulkunāya Namaḥ.
ॐ ह्रीं फल्गुणाय नम: |	Om Hrīm Phalguṇāya Namaḥ.
ॐ ह्रीं फणानाथाय नम: |	Om Hrīm Phaṇānātāya Namaḥ.
ॐ ह्रीं फणश्राय नम: |	Om Hrīm Phaṇēśāya Namaḥ.
ॐ ह्रीं फणिरक्षकाय नम: |	Om Hrīm Phaṇirakṣakāya Namaḥ.
ॐ ह्रीं फणीपतय नम: |	Om Hrīm Phaṇīpatayē Namaḥ.
ॐ ह्रीं फणीशानाय नम: |	Om Hrīm Phaṇīśānāya Namaḥ.
ॐ ह्रीं फणराजाय नम: |	Om Hrīm Phaṇārājāya Namaḥ.
ॐ ह्रीं फणालिन्दाय नम: |	Om Hrīm Phaṇāḷindāya Namaḥ.
ॐ ह्रीं फणाकृतय नम: |	Om Hrīm Phaṇākru'tayē Namaḥ.
ॐ ह्रीं बलभद्राय नम: | 290	Om Hrīm Balabhadrāya Namaḥ.
ॐ ह्रीं बलिन नम: |	Om Hrīm Baliṉē Namaḥ.
ॐ ह्रीं बलधियश्रम: |	Om Hrīm Baladhiyē Namaḥ.
ॐ ह्रीं बलवर्धनाय नम: |	Om Hrīm Balavardhanāya Namaḥ.
ॐ ह्रीं बलप्राणाय नम: |	Om Hrīm Balaprāṇāya Namaḥ.
ॐ ह्रीं बलाधीशाय नम: |	Om Hrīm Balādhīśāya Namaḥ.

ॐ ह्रीं बलिदान प्रियङ्कराय नम:		Om Hrīm Balidāna Priyaṅkarāya Namaḥ.
ॐ ह्रीं बलिराजाय नम:		Om Hrīm Balirājāya Namaḥ.
ॐ ह्रीं बलिप्राणाय नम:		Om Hrīm Baliprāṇō Namaḥ.
ॐ ह्रीं बलिनाथाय नम:		Om Hrīm Balināthāya Namaḥ.
ॐ ह्रीं बलिप्रभवञ्ज्ञम:	300	Om Hrīm Baliprabhuvē Namaḥ.
ॐ ह्रीं बलीयाय नम:		Om Hrīm Balīyāya Namaḥ.
ॐ ह्रीं बलाय नम:		Om Hrīm Balāya Namaḥ.
ॐ ह्रीं बालक्ष्राय नम:		Om Hrīm Bālēśāya Namaḥ.
ॐ ह्रीं बालकाय नम:		Om Hrīm Bālakāya Namaḥ.
ॐ ह्रीं प्रिय दर्शनाय नम:		Om Hrīm Priya Darśanāya Namaḥ.
ॐ ह्रीं भद्रिणे नम:		Om Hrīm Bhadriṇē Namaḥ.
ॐ ह्रीं भद्रप्र दाय नम:		Om Hrīm Bhadra Pradāya Namaḥ.
ॐ ह्रीं भीमाय नम:		Om Hrīm Bhīmāya Namaḥ.
ॐ ह्रीं भीमसञ्ज्ञाय नम:		Om Hrīm Bhīmasēnāya Namaḥ.
ॐ ह्रीं भयङ्कराय नम:	310	Om Hrīm Bhayaṅkarāya Namaḥ.
ॐ ह्रीं भव्याय नम:		Om Hrīm Bhavyāya Namaḥ.
ॐ ह्रीं भव्य प्रियाय नम:		Om Hrīm Bhavya Priyāya Namaḥ.
ॐ ह्रीं भूतपतयञ्ज्ञम:		Om Hrīm Bhūtapatayē Namaḥ.
ॐ ह्रीं भूतविनाशकाय नम:		Om Hrīm Bhūtavināśakāya Namaḥ.
ॐ ह्रीं भूतञ्ज्ञाय नम:		Om Hrīm Bhūtēśāya Namaḥ.
ॐ ह्रीं भूतिदाय नम:		Om Hrīm Bhūtidāya Namaḥ.

ॐ ह्रीं भर्गाय नम:		Om Hrīm BhargāYa Namaḥ.
ॐ ह्रीं भूतभव्याय नम:		Om Hrīm Bhūtabhavyāya Namaḥ.
ॐ ह्रीं भव्रेश्वराय नम:		Om Hrīm Bhavrēśvarāya Namaḥ.
ॐ ह्रीं भवानीशाय नम:	320	Om Hrīm Bhavānīśāya Namaḥ.
ॐ ह्रीं भवानी नायकाय नम:|	Om Hrīm Bhavānī Nāyakāya Namaḥ.
ॐ ह्रीं भवाय नम:		Om Hrīm Bhavāya Namaḥ.
ॐ ह्रीं मकाराय नम:		Om Hrīm Makārāya Namaḥ.
ॐ ह्रीं माधवाय नम:		Om Hrīm Mādhavāya Namaḥ.
ॐ ह्रीं मानिन नम:		Om Hrīm Māṉiṉē Namaḥ.
ॐ ह्रीं मीनकेतवभ्राम:		Om Hrīm Mīnakētavē Namaḥ.
ॐ ह्रीं महेश्वराय नम:		Om Hrīm Mahēśvarāya Namaḥ.
ॐ ह्रीं महर्षियभ्राम:		Om Hrīm Mahariṣiyē Namaḥ.
ॐ ह्रीं मदनाय नम:		Om Hrīm Madanāya Namaḥ.
ॐ ह्रीं मन्थाय नम:	330	Om Hrīm Manthāya Namaḥ.
ॐ ह्रीं मिथुनेश्राय नम:		Om Hrīm Mithunēśāya Namaḥ.
ॐ ह्रीं अमराधिपाय नम:		Om Hrīm Amarādhipāya Namaḥ.
ॐ ह्रीं मरीचयभ्राम:		Om Hrīm Marīcayē Namaḥ.
ॐ ह्रीं मञ्जुलाय नम:		Om Hrīm Mañjulāya Namaḥ.
ॐ ह्रीं मोहाय नम:		Om Hrīm Mōhāya Namaḥ.

ॐ ह्रीं मोहग्नभ्राम:		Om Hrīm Mōhagne Namaḥ.
ॐ ह्रीं मोहमर्दनाय नम:		Om Hrīm Mōha Mardanāya Namaḥ.
ॐ ह्रीं मोहकाय नम:		Om Hrīm Mōhakāya Namaḥ.
ॐ ह्रीं मोहनाय नम:		Om Hrīm Mōhanāya Namaḥ.
ॐ ह्रीं मभ्राप्रियाय नम:	340	Om Hrīm Mēdhāpriyāya Namaḥ. 340
ॐ ह्रीं मोह विनाशकाय नम:	Om Hrīm Mōha Vināśakāya Namaḥ.
ॐ ह्रीं महीपतये नम:		Om Hrīm Mahīpatayē Namaḥ.
ॐ ह्रीं महश्रानाय नम:		Om Hrīm Mahēśānāya Namaḥ.
ॐ ह्रीं महाराजाय नम:		Om Hrīm Mahārājāya Namaḥ.
ॐ ह्रीं महश्रराय नम:		Om Hrīm Mahēśvarāya Namaḥ.
ॐ ह्रीं मनोहराय नम:		Om Hrīm Manōharāya Namaḥ.
ॐ ह्रीं महीश्वराय नम:		Om Hrīm Mahīśvarāya Namaḥ.
ॐ ह्रीं महीपालाय नम:		Om Hrīm Mahīpālāya Namaḥ.
ॐ ह्रीं महीनाथाय नम:		Om Hrīm MahīnāthāYa Namaḥ.
ॐ ह्रीं महीप्रियाय नम:	350	Om Hrīm Mahīpriyāya Namaḥ.
ॐ ह्रीं महीधराय नम:		Om Hrīm Mahīdharāya Namaḥ.
ॐ ह्रीं महादश्राय नम:		Om Hrīm Mahādēvāya Namaḥ.
ॐ ह्रीं महीशानाय नम:		Om Hrīm Mahīśānāya Namaḥ.

ॐ ह्रीं मनुराजाय नम:		Om Hrīm Manurājāya Namaḥ.
ॐ ह्रीं मधुराजाय नम:		Om Hrīm Madhurājāya Namaḥ.
ॐ ह्रीं मुनिप्रियाय नम:		Om Hrīm Munipriyāya Namaḥ.
ॐ ह्रीं मौनीन नम:		Om Hrīm Mauṇiṇē Namaḥ.
ॐ ह्रीं मौनधराय नम:		Om Hrīm Maunadharāya Namaḥ.
ॐ ह्रीं मभ्राय नम:		Om Hrīm Mēdhāya Namaḥ.
ॐ ह्रीं मन्दराय नम:	360	Om Hrīm Mandarāya Namaḥ.
ॐ ह्रीं मतिवर्धनाय नम:		Om Hrīm Mativardhanāya Namaḥ.
ॐ ह्रीं मतिदाय नम:		Om Hrīm Matidāya Namaḥ.
ॐ ह्रीं मन्धराय नम:		Om Hrīm Mandharāya Namaḥ.
ॐ ह्रीं मत्राय नम:		Om Hrīm Mantrāya Namaḥ.
ॐ ह्रीं मन्त्रीशाय नम:		Om Hrīm Mantrīśāya Namaḥ.
ॐ ह्रीं मन्त्र नायकाय नम:		Om Hrīm Mantra Nāyakāya Namaḥ.
ॐ ह्रीं मभ्राविन नम:		Om Hrīm Mēdhāviṇē Namaḥ.
ॐ ह्रीं मानदाय नम:		Om Hrīm Mānadāya Namaḥ.
ॐ ह्रीं मानिन नम:		Om Hrīm Māṇiṇē Namaḥ.
ॐ ह्रीं मानग्नभ्राम:	370	Om Hrīm Mānagṇē Namaḥ.
ॐ ह्रीं मानमर्दनाय नम:		Om Hrīm Mānamardanāya Namaḥ.

ॐ ह्रीं मीनगाय नमः।	Om Hrīm Mīnagāya Namaḥ.
ॐ ह्रीं मकराधीशाय नमः।	Om Hrīm Makarādhīśāya Namaḥ.
ॐ ह्रीं मधुराय नमः।	Om Hrīm Madhurāya Namaḥ.
ॐ ह्रीं मकराय नमः।	Om Hrīm Makarāya Namaḥ.
ॐ ह्रीं मणि रञ्जिताय नमः।	Om Hrīm Maṇi Rañjitāya Namaḥ.
ॐ ह्रीं मणि रम्भाय नमः।	Om Hrīm Maṇi Ramyāya Namaḥ.
ॐ ह्रीं मणि भ्रात्र नमः।	Om Hrīm Maṇi Bhrātrē Namaḥ.
ॐ ह्रीं मणिमण्डल मण्डिताय नमः।	Om Hrīm Maṇi Maṇḍala Maṇḍitāya Namaḥ.
ॐ ह्रीं मन्त्रिणभ्राम्। 380	Om Hrīm Mantriṇē Namaḥ.
ॐ ह्रीं मन्त्रदाय नमः।	Om Hrīm Mantradāya Namaḥ.
ॐ ह्रीं मुग्धाय नमः।	Om Hrīm Mugdhāya Namaḥ.
ॐ ह्रीं मोक्षदाय नमः।	Om Hrīm Mōkṣadāya Namaḥ.
ॐ ह्रीं मोक्ष वल्लभाय नमः।	Om Hrīm Mōkṣa Vallabhāya Namaḥ.
ॐ ह्रीं मल्लाय नमः।	Om Hrīm Mallāya Namaḥ.
ॐ ह्रीं मल्ल प्रियाय नमः।	Om Hrīm Malla Priyāya Namaḥ.
ॐ ह्रीं मल्लकाय नमः।	Om Hrīm Mallakāya Namaḥ.
ॐ ह्रीं मझ्झन प्रभवभ्राम्।	Om Hrīm Mēlana Prabhavē Namaḥ.
ॐ ह्रीं मल्लिका माला दराय नमः।	Om Hrīm Mallikā Mālā Darāya Namaḥ.
ॐ ह्रीं मल्लिका गन्ध रमणाय नमः। 390	Om Hrīm Mallikā Gandha Ramaṇāya Namaḥ. 390

ॐ ह्रीं मालती कुसुम प्रभव नम:।	Om Hrīm Mālatī Kusuma Prabhavē Namaḥ.
ॐ ह्रीं मालतीशाय नम: ।	Om Hrīm Mālatīśāya Namaḥ.
ॐ ह्रीं मघानाथाय नम: ।	Om Hrīm Maghānātāya Namaḥ.
ॐ ह्रीं मघाधीशाय नम: ।	Om Hrīm Maghādhīśāya Namaḥ.
ॐ ह्रीं मोघ मूर्तये नम: ।	Om Hrīm Māgha Mūrtayē Namaḥ.
ॐ ह्रीं मघश्वराय नम: ।	Om Hrīm Maghēśvarāya Namaḥ.
ॐ ह्रीं मूलाभाय नम: ।	Om Hrīm Mūlābhāya Namaḥ.
ॐ ह्रीं मूलग्न नम: ।	Om Hrīm Mūlagnē Namaḥ.
ॐ ह्रीं मूलाय नम: ।	Om Hrīm Mūlāya Namaḥ.
ॐ ह्रीं मूलदाय नम: । 400	Om Hrīm Mūladāya Namaḥ. 400
ॐ ह्रीं मूलसम्भवाय नम: ।	Om Hrīm Mūla Sambhavāya Namaḥ.
ॐ ह्रीं माणिक्यरोचिषे नम: ।	Om Hrīm Māṇikyarōciṣē Namaḥ.
ॐ ह्रीं सम्मुधाय नम: ।	Om Hrīm Sam'mugdhāya Namaḥ.
ॐ ह्रीं मणि कूटाय नम: ।	Om Hrīm Maṇi Kūṭāya Namaḥ.
ॐ ह्रीं मणि प्रियाय नम: ।	Om Hrīm Maṇi Priyāya Namaḥ.
ॐ ह्रीं मुकुन्दाय नम: ।	Om Hrīm Mukundāya Namaḥ.
ॐ ह्रीं मदनाय नम: ।	Om Hrīm Madanāya Namaḥ.
ॐ ह्रीं मन्दाय नम: ।	Om Hrīm Mandāya Namaḥ.
ॐ ह्रीं मदवन्द्याय नम: ।	Om Hrīm Madavandyāya Namaḥ.
ॐ ह्रीं मनुप्रभवश्रम: । 410	Om Hrīm Manuprabhavē Namaḥ.

ॐ ह्रीं मनस्थाय नम:		Om Hrīm Manas'sthāya Namaḥ.
ॐ ह्रीं मङ्काधीशाय नम:		Om Hrīm Mēnakādhīśāya Namaḥ.
ॐ ह्रीं मङ्का प्रिय दर्शनाय नम:		Om Hrīm Mēnakā Priya Darśanāya Namaḥ.
ॐ ह्रीं यामाय नम:		Om Hrīm Yāmāya Namaḥ.
ॐ ह्रीं अयामाय नम:		Om Hrīm Ayāmāya Namaḥ.
ॐ ह्रीं यामलाय नम:		Om Hrīm Yāmalāya Namaḥ.
ॐ ह्रीं यमिदेव्राय नम:		Om Hrīm Yamidēvāya Namaḥ.
ॐ ह्रीं यादवाय नम:		Om Hrīm Yādavāya Namaḥ.
ॐ ह्रीं यदुनायकाय नम:		Om Hrīm Yadunāyakāya Namaḥ.
ॐ ह्रीं याचकाय नम:	420	Om Hrīm Yācakāya Namaḥ. 420
ॐ ह्रीं यज्ञकाय नम:		Om Hrīm Yajñakāya Namaḥ.
ॐ ह्रीं यज्ञाय नम:		Om Hrīm Yajñāya Namaḥ.
ॐ ह्रीं यज्ञेश्राय नम:		Om Hrīm Yajñēśāya Namaḥ.
ॐ ह्रीं यज्ञवर्धनाय नम:		Om Hrīm Yajña Vardhanāya Namaḥ.
ॐ ह्रीं रमापतय नम:		Om Hrīm Ramāpatayē Namaḥ.
ॐ ह्रीं रमाधीशाय नम:		Om Hrīm Ramādhīśāya Namaḥ.
ॐ ह्रीं रमेश्राय नम:		Om Hrīm Ramēśāya Namaḥ.
ॐ ह्रीं रामवल्लभाय नम:		Om Hrīm Rāmavallabhāya Namaḥ.
ॐ ह्रीं रमानाथाय नम:		Om Hrīm Ramānāthāya Namaḥ.
ॐ ह्रीं रमा कान्ताय नम:	430	Om Hrīm Ramā Kāntāya Namaḥ.

ॐ ह्रीं रमेश्वराय नम:		Om Hrīm Ramēśvarāya Namaḥ.
ॐ ह्रीं रेवती रमणाय नम:		Om Hrīm Rēvatī Ramaṇāya Namaḥ.
ॐ ह्रीं रामाय नम:		Om Hrīm Rāmāya Namaḥ.
ॐ ह्रीं रामनन्दनाय नम:		Om Hrīm Rāmanandanāya Namaḥ.
ॐ ह्रीं रम्यमूर्तय नम:		Om Hrīm Ramyamūrtayē Namaḥ.
ॐ ह्रीं रतीशानाय नम:		Om Hrīm Ratīśānāya Namaḥ.
ॐ ह्रीं राकाया नायकाय नम:		Om Hrīm Rākāyā Nāyakāya Namaḥ.
ॐ ह्रीं रवयभ्राम:		Om Hrīm Ravayē Namaḥ.
ॐ ह्रीं लक्ष्मीधराय नम:		Om Hrīm Lakṣmīdharāya Namaḥ.
ॐ ह्रीं ललज्जिह्वाय नम:	440	Om Hrīm Lalajjihvāya Namaḥ.
ॐ ह्रीं लक्ष्मी बीज जपाय नम:		Om Hrīm Lakṣmī Bīja Japāya Namaḥ.
ॐ ह्रीं लाम्पटाय नम:		Om Hrīm Lampaṭāya Namaḥ.
ॐ ह्रीं लम्ब राजश्राय नम:		Om Hrīm Lambarājēśāya Namaḥ.
ॐ ह्रीं लम्बोदराय नम:		Om Hrīm Lambadēśāya Namaḥ.
ॐ ह्रीं लकारभुव नम:		Om Hrīm Lakārabhuvē Namaḥ.
ॐ ह्रीं वाम वल्लभाय नम:		Om Hrīm Vāma Vallabhāya Namaḥ.
ॐ ह्रीं वन्द्याय नम:		Om Hrīm Vandyāya Namaḥ.
ॐ ह्रीं वनमालिन नम:		Om Hrīm Vanamāliṇē Namaḥ.
ॐ ह्रीं वलश्राय नम:		Om Hrīm Valēśvarāya Namaḥ.
ॐ ह्रीं वशस्थाय नम:	450	Om Hrīm Vaśasthāya Namaḥ.
ॐ ह्रीं वनगाय नम:		Om Hrīm Vanagāya Namaḥ.

ॐ ह्रीं वन्ध्याय नम:		Om Hrīm Vandhyāya Namaḥ.
ॐ ह्रीं वनराजाय नम:		Om Hrīm Vanarājāya Namaḥ.
ॐ ह्रीं वनाह्वयाय नम:		Om Hrīm Vanāhvayāya Namaḥ.
ॐ ह्रीं वनचराय नम:		Om Hrīm Vanacarāya Namaḥ.
ॐ ह्रीं वनाधीशाय नम:		Om Hrīm Vanādhīśāya Namaḥ.
ॐ ह्रीं वनमाला विभूषणाय नम:	Om Hrīm Vanamālā Vibhūṣaṇāya Namaḥ.
ॐ ह्रीं वेणुप्रियाय नम:		Om Hrīm Vēṇupriyāya Namaḥ.
ॐ ह्रीं वनाकाराय नम:		Om Hrīm Vanākārāya Namaḥ.
ॐ ह्रीं वनराध्याय नम:	460	Om Hrīm Vanarādhyāya Namaḥ.
ॐ ह्रीं वनप्रभवऋम:		Om Hrīm Vanaprabhavē Namaḥ.
ॐ ह्रीं शम्भव नम:		Om Hrīm Śambhavē Namaḥ.
ॐ ह्रीं शङ्कर सन्तुष्टाय नम:		Om Hrīm Śaṅkara Santuṣṭāya Namaḥ.
ॐ ह्रीं शम्बराराय नम:		Om Hrīm Śambarārayē Namaḥ.
ॐ ह्रीं सराचराय नम:		Om Hrīm Sarācarāya Namaḥ.
ॐ ह्रीं सनातनाय नम:		Om Hrīm Sanātanāya Namaḥ.
ॐ ह्रीं शबरी प्रणताय नम:		Om Hrīm Śabarī Praṇatāya Namaḥ.
ॐ ह्रीं शालाय नम:		Om Hrīm Śālāya Namaḥ.
ॐ ह्रीं शिली मुख ध्वनि प्रियाय नम:		Om Hrīm Śilī Mukha Dhvani Priyāya Namaḥ.
ॐ ह्रीं शकुलाय नम:	470	Om Hrīm Śakulāya Namaḥ. 470
ॐ ह्रीं शल्ल्काय नम:		Om Hrīm Śallkāya Namaḥ.
ॐ ह्रीं शीलाय नम:		Om Hrīm Śīlāya Namaḥ.

ॐ ह्रीं शीतरश्मय नम:		Om Hrīm Śītiraśmayē Namaḥ.
ॐ ह्रीं सीतांशुकाय नम:		Om Hrīm Sītāmśukāya Namaḥ.
ॐ ह्रीं शीलदाय नम:		Om Hrīm Śīladāya Namaḥ.
ॐ ह्रीं शीकराय नम:		Om Hrīm Śīkarāya Namaḥ.
ॐ ह्रीं शीलाय नम:		Om Hrīm Śīlāya Namaḥ.
ॐ ह्रीं शीलशीलिन नम:		Om Hrīm Śālīśīlinē Namaḥ.
ॐ ह्रीं शनैश्वराय नम:		Om Hrīm Śanaiścarāya Namaḥ.
ॐ ह्रीं सिद्धाय नम:	480	Om Hrīm Siddhāya Namaḥ. 480
ॐ ह्रीं सिद्धिकराय नम:		Om Hrīm Siddhikarāya Namaḥ.
ॐ ह्रीं साध्याय नम:		Om Hrīm Sādhyāya Namaḥ.
ॐ ह्रीं सिद्धिभुव नम:		Om Hrīm Siddhibhuvē Namaḥ.
ॐ ह्रीं सिद्धिभावनाय नम:		Om Hrīm Siddhi Bhāvanāya Namaḥ.
ॐ ह्रीं सिद्धान्त वल्लभाय नम:		Om Hrīm Siddhānta Vallabhāya Namaḥ.
ॐ ह्रीं सिन्धुव नम:		Om Hrīm Sindhuvē Namaḥ.
ॐ ह्रीं सिन्धुतीर निषष्वकाय नम:		Om Hrīm Sindhutīra Niṣēvakāya Namaḥ.
ॐ ह्रीं सिन्धु पतय नम:		Om Hrīm Sindhu Patayē Namaḥ.
ॐ ह्रीं सुराधीशाय नम:		Om Hrīm Surādhīśāya Namaḥ.
ॐ ह्रीं सरश्रीराय नम:	490	Om Hrīm Sarēdhīrāya Namaḥ.
ॐ ह्रीं सरसिरुह लोचनाय नम:		Om Hrīm Sarasīruha Lōcanāya Namaḥ.
ॐ ह्रीं सरित्पतयभ्रम:		Om Hrīm Saritpatayē Namaḥ.
ॐ ह्रीं सरित्संस्थाय नम:		Om Hrīm Sarit Samsthāya Namaḥ.

ॐ ह्रीं सरतराय नम:		Om Hrīm Saratarāya Namaḥ.
ॐ ह्रीं सिन्धुव नम:		Om Hrīm Sindhuvē Namaḥ.
ॐ ह्रीं सरोवराय नम:		Om Hrīm Sarōvarāya Namaḥ.
ॐ ह्रीं सखाय नम:		Om Hrīm Sakhāya Namaḥ.
ॐ ह्रीं वीरपतय नम:		Om Hrīm Vīrapatayē Namaḥ.
ॐ ह्रीं सूताय नम:		Om Hrīm Sūtāya Namaḥ.
ॐ ह्रीं सचेतसे नम:	500	Om Hrīm Sacētasē Namaḥ. 500
ॐ ह्रीं सत्पतय नम:		Om Hrīm Satpatayē Namaḥ.
ॐ ह्रीं सतिताय नम:		Om Hrīm Satitāya Namaḥ.
ॐ ह्रीं सिन्धुराज सदाभूज्याय नम:		Om Hrīm Sindhurāja Sadābhūjyāya Namaḥ.
ॐ ह्रीं सदाशिवाय नम:		Om Hrīm Sadāśivāya Namaḥ.
ॐ ह्रीं सताङ्गतय नम:		Om Hrīm Satāṅgatayē Namaḥ.
ॐ ह्रीं सदृशाय नम:		Om Hrīm Sadru'śāya Namaḥ.
ॐ ह्रीं सहसाय नम:		Om Hrīm Sāhasāya Namaḥ.
ॐ ह्रीं शूर सेव्य मानाय नम:		Om Hrīm Śūra Sēvya Mānāya Namaḥ.
ॐ ह्रीं सतीपतय नम:		Om Hrīm Satīpataye Namaḥ.
ॐ ह्रीं सूर्याय नम:	510	Om Hrīm Sūryāya Namaḥ. 510
ॐ ह्रीं सूर्यपतय नम:		Om Hrīm Sūryapatayē Namaḥ.
ॐ ह्रीं सेव्याय नम:		Om Hrīm Sēvyāya Namaḥ.
ॐ ह्रीं सेवाप्रियाय नम:		Om Hrīm Sēvāpriyāya Namaḥ.
ॐ ह्रीं सनातनाय नम:		Om Hrīm Sanātanāya Namaḥ.

ॐ ह्रीं सनीशाय नम:		Om Hrīm Sanīśāya Namaḥ.
ॐ ह्रीं शशिनाथाय नम:		Om Hrīm Śaśināthāya Namaḥ.
ॐ ह्रीं सतीसक्ष्याय नम:		Om Hrīm Satīsēvyāya Namaḥ.
ॐ ह्रीं सतीरताय नम:		Om Hrīm Satīratāya Namaḥ.
ॐ ह्रीं सतीप्राणाय नम:		Om Hrīm Satīprāṇāya Namaḥ.
ॐ ह्रीं सतीनाथाय नम:	520	Om Hrīm Satīnāthāya Namaḥ.
ॐ ह्रीं सतीश्वराय नम:		Om Hrīm Satīśvarāya Namaḥ.
ॐ ह्रीं सिद्धराजाय नम:		Om Hrīm Siddharājāya Namaḥ.
ॐ ह्रीं सतीतुष्टाय नम:		Om Hrīm Satītuṣṭāya Namaḥ.
ॐ ह्रीं सचिवाय नम:		Om Hrīm Sacivāya Namaḥ.
ॐ ह्रीं सव्य वाहनाय नम:		Om Hrīm Savya Vāhanāya Namaḥ.
ॐ ह्रीं सती नायकाय नम:		Om Hrīm Satī Nāyakāya Namaḥ.
ॐ ह्रीं सन्तुष्टाय नम:		Om Hrīm Santuṣṭāya Namaḥ.
ॐ ह्रीं सव्यसाचिन नम:		Om Hrīm Savyasācinē Namaḥ.
ॐ ह्रीं समन्तकाय नम:		Om Hrīm Samantakāya Namaḥ.
ॐ ह्रीं सच्चित्ताय नम:	530	Om Hrīm Saccittāya Namaḥ.
ॐ ह्रीं सर्वसन्तोषाय नम:		Om Hrīm Sarva Santōṣāya Namaḥ.
ॐ ह्रीं सर्वाराधनाय नम:		Om Hrīm Sarvārādhanāya Namaḥ.
ॐ ह्रीं सुसिद्धिदाय नम:		Om Hrīm Susiddhidāya Namaḥ.
ॐ ह्रीं सर्वाराध्याय नम:		Om Hrīm Sarvārādhyāya Namaḥ.
ॐ ह्रीं शचीवाक्याय नम:		Om Hrīm Śacīvākyāya Namaḥ.
ॐ ह्रीं सागराय नम:		Om Hrīm Sāgarāya Namaḥ.
ॐ ह्रीं सगराय नम:		Om Hrīm Sagarāya Namaḥ.

ॐ ह्रीं साद्धय नम:		Om Hrīm Sārdhāya Namaḥ.
ॐ ह्रीं समुद्राय नम:		Om Hrīm Samudrāya Namaḥ.
ॐ ह्रीं सर्व प्रिय दर्शनाय नम:	540	Om Hrīm Sarva Priya Darśanāya Namaḥ. 540
ॐ ह्रीं समुद्रेश्राय नम:		Om Hrīm Samudrēśāya Namaḥ.
ॐ ह्रीं सर्वमूर्ति स्वरूपाय नम:		Om Hrīm Sarvamūrti Svarūpāya Namaḥ.
ॐ ह्रीं सरोनाताय नम:		Om Hrīm Sarōnātāya Namaḥ.
ॐ ह्रीं सरसी जलदा काराय नम:		Om Hrīm Sarasī Jaladā Kārāya Namaḥ.
ॐ ह्रीं सरसी जलदार्चिताय नम:		Om Hrīm Sarasī Jaladārcitāya Namaḥ.
ॐ ह्रीं सामुद्रिकाय नम:		Om Hrīm Sāmudrikāya Namaḥ.
ॐ ह्रीं समुद्रात्मन नम:		Om Hrīm Samudrātmaṇē Namaḥ.
ॐ ह्रीं सव्य मानाय नम:		Om Hrīm Sēvya Mānāya Namaḥ.
ॐ ह्रीं सुरेश्राय नम:		Om Hrīm Surēśvarāya Namaḥ.
ॐ ह्रीं सुरसव्याय नम:	550	Om Hrīm Surasēvyāya Namaḥ.
ॐ ह्रीं सुरेशानाय नम:		Om Hrīm Surēśānāya Namaḥ.
ॐ ह्रीं सुरनाथाय नम:		Om Hrīm Suranāthāya Namaḥ.
ॐ ह्रीं सुरेश्राय नम:		Om Hrīm Surēśvarāya Namaḥ.
ॐ ह्रीं सुराध्याय नम:		Om Hrīm Surādhyakṣāya Namaḥ.
ॐ ह्रीं सुराराध्याय नम:		Om Hrīm Surārādhyāya Namaḥ.
ॐ ह्रीं सुरबृन्द विशारदाय नम:		Om Hrīm Surabru'ndaya Viśāradāya Namaḥ.
ॐ ह्रीं सुरश्रेष्ठाय नम:		Om Hrīm Suraśrēṣṭhāya Namaḥ.

ॐ ह्रीं सुरप्राणाय नम:		Om Hrīm Suraprāṇāya Namaḥ.
ॐ ह्रीं सुरसिन्धु निवासिने नम:		Om Hrīm Surasindhuya Nivāsināya Namaḥ.
ॐ ह्रीं सुधा प्रियाय नम:	560	Om Hrīm Sudhāya Priyāya Namaḥ. 560

ॐ ह्रीं सुधा धीशाय नम:		Om Hrīm Sudhāya Dhīśāya Namaḥ.
ॐ ह्रीं सुधा राध्याय नम:		Om Hrīm Sudhāya Sādhyāya Namaḥ.
ॐ ह्रीं सुधा पतय नम:		Om Hrīm Sudhāya Pataye Namaḥ.
ॐ ह्रीं सुधा नाथाय नम:		Om Hrīm Sudhāya Nāthāya Namaḥ.
ॐ ह्रीं सुधा भूताय नम:		Om Hrīm Sudhāya Bhūtāya Namaḥ.
ॐ ह्रीं सुधा सागर सक्षिताय नम:		Om Hrīm Sudhāya Sāgaraya Sēvitāya Namaḥ.
ॐ ह्रीं हाटकाय नम:		Om Hrīm Hāṭakāya Namaḥ.
ॐ ह्रीं हीरकाय नम:		Om Hrīm Hīrakāya Namaḥ.
ॐ ह्रीं हन्त्र नम:		Om Hrīm Hantrēya Namaḥ.
ॐ ह्रीं रुचिरप्रभाय नम:	570	Om Hrīm Ruciraprabhavēya Namaḥ. 570

ॐ ह्रीं हव्यवाहनाय नम:		Om Hrīm Havyavāhaṇāya Namaḥ.
ॐ ह्रीं हरिद्राभाय नम:		Om Hrīm Haridrābhāya Namaḥ.
ॐ ह्रीं हरिद्रारस मर्दनाय नम:		Om Hrīm Haridrārasaya Mardanāya Namaḥ.
ॐ ह्रीं हेतिराजाय नम:		Om Hrīm Hētirājāya Namaḥ.
ॐ ह्रीं हेतवे नम:		Om Hrīm Hētavē Namaḥ.

ॐ ह्रीं हरये नम:		Om Hrīm Harayē Namaḥ.
ॐ ह्रीं हरिधात्रभ्राम:		Om Hrīm Haritātrēya Namaḥ.
ॐ ह्रीं हरिनाथाय नम:		Om Hrīm Harināthāya Namaḥ.
ॐ ह्रीं हरिप्रियाय नम:		Om Hrīm Haripriyāya Namaḥ.
ॐ ह्रीं हरिपूज्याय नम:	580	Om Hrīm Haripūjyāya Namaḥ.

ॐ ह्रीं हरिप्राणाय नम:		Om Hrīm Hariprāṇāya Namaḥ.
ॐ ह्रीं हरिहृष्टाय नम:		Om Hrīm Harihru'ṣṭāya Namaḥ.
ॐ ह्रीं हरीन्द्रकाय नम:		Om Hrīm Haridrakāya Namaḥ.
ॐ ह्रीं हरीशाय नम:		Om Hrīm Harīśāya Namaḥ.
ॐ ह्रीं हन्त्रिकाय नम:		Om Hrīm Harīntrakāya Namaḥ.
ॐ ह्रीं हीराय नम:		Om Hrīm Hīrīśāya Namaḥ.
ॐ ह्रीं हरिनाम परायणाय नम:		Om Hrīm Harināmaya Parāyaṇāya Namaḥ.
ॐ ह्रीं हरिमुग्धाय नम:		Om Hrīm Harimugdhāya Namaḥ.
ॐ ह्रीं हरीरम्याय नम:		Om Hrīm Harīramyāya Namaḥ.
ॐ ह्रीं हरिदासाय नम:	590	Om Hrīm Haridāsāya Namaḥ. 590

ॐ ह्रीं हरीश्वराय नम:		Om Hrīm Harīśvarāya Namaḥ.
ॐ ह्रीं हराय नम:		Om Hrīm Harāya Namaḥ.
ॐ ह्रीं हरिपतयभ्राम:		Om Hrīm Haripatayē Namaḥ.
ॐ ह्रीं हाराय नम:		Om Hrīm Hārāya Namaḥ.
ॐ ह्रीं हरिणी चित्त हारकाय नम:		Om Hrīm Hariṇī Citta Hārakāya Namaḥ.
ॐ ह्रीं हिताय नम:		Om Hrīm Hitāya Namaḥ.

ॐ ह्रीं हरप्राणाय नमः		Om Hrīm Hara Prāṇāya Namaḥ.
ॐ ह्रीं हरि वाहनाय नमः		Om Hrīm Hari Vāhanāya Namaḥ.
ॐ ह्रीं हंस वाहनाय नमः		Om Hrīm Hamsa Vāhanāya Namaḥ.
ॐ ह्रीं हंसाय नमः	600	Om Hrīm Hamsāya Namaḥ. 600
ॐ ह्रीं हंस प्रियाय नमः		Om Hrīm Hamsa Priyāya Namaḥ.
ॐ ह्रीं हुंहुं मन्त्र प्रियाय नमः		Om Hrīm Humhum Mantra Priyāya Namaḥ.
ॐ ह्रीं हरिहराय नमः		Om Hrīm Hariharāya Namaḥ.
ॐ ह्रीं हुतवाहनाय नमः		Om Hrīm Hutavāhanāya Namaḥ.
ॐ ह्रीं हुताशनाय नमः		Om Hrīm Hutāśanāya Namaḥ.
ॐ ह्रीं हलिन नमः		Om Hrīm Haliṇē Namaḥ.
ॐ ह्रीं हक्काय नमः		Om Hrīm Hakkāya Namaḥ.
ॐ ह्रीं हालाय नमः		Om Hrīm Hālāya Namaḥ.
ॐ ह्रीं हलहलायुधाय नमः		Om Hrīm Hala Halāyudhaya Namaḥ.
ॐ ह्रीं हलाकाराय नमः	610	Om Hrīm Halākārāya Namaḥ. 610
ॐ ह्रीं हलीशानाय नमः		Om Hrīm Halīśānāya Namaḥ.
ॐ ह्रीं हलिपूज्याय नमः		Om Hrīm Halipūjyāya Namaḥ.
ॐ ह्रीं हलिप्रियाय नमः		Om Hrīm Halipriyāya Namaḥ.
ॐ ह्रीं हरपुत्राय नमः		Om Hrīm Haraputrāya Namaḥ.
ॐ ह्रीं हरोत्साहाय नमः		Om Hrīm Harōtsāhō Namaḥ.
ॐ ह्रीं हरसूनवभ्राम		Om Hrīm Harasūnuvē Namaḥ.
ॐ ह्रीं हरात्मजाय नमः		Om Hrīm Harātmajāya Namaḥ.
ॐ ह्रीं हरबन्धव नमः		Om Hrīm Harabandhuvē Namaḥ.

ॐ ह्रीं हराधीशाय नम:		Om Hrīm Harādhīśāya Namaḥ.
ॐ ह्रीं हरान्तकाय नम:	620	Om Hrīm Harāntakāya Namaḥ.
ॐ ह्रीं हराकृतय नम:		Om Hrīm Harākru'tayē Namaḥ.
ॐ ह्रीं हरप्राणाय नम:		Om Hrīm Haraprāṇāya Namaḥ.
ॐ ह्रीं हरमान्याय नम:		Om Hrīm Haramān'yāya Namaḥ.
ॐ ह्रीं हरवैरि विनाशनाय नम:		Om Hrīm Haravairi Vināśanāya Namaḥ.
ॐ ह्रीं हरशत्रु हराय नम:		Om Hrīm Haraśatru Harāya Namaḥ.
ॐ ह्रीं हररूपधराय नम:		Om Hrīm Hararūpadharāya Namaḥ.
ॐ ह्रीं हुङ्कराय नम:		Om Hrīm Huṅkārāya Namaḥ.
ॐ ह्रीं हरिणी प्रियाय नम:		Om Hrīm Hariṇī Priyāya Namaḥ.
ॐ ह्रीं हाटकेशाय नम:		Om Hrīm Hāṭakēśāya Namaḥ.
ॐ ह्रीं हरेशानाय नम:	630	Om Hrīm Harēśānāya Namaḥ.
ॐ ह्रीं हाटक प्रिय दर्शनाय नम:		Om Hrīm Hāṭaka Priya Darśanāya Namaḥ.
ॐ ह्रीं हाट कप्राणाय नम:		Om Hrīm Hāṭaka Prāṇāya Namaḥ.
ॐ ह्रीं हाट भूषण भूषकाय नम:		Om Hrīm Hāṭa Bhūṣaṇa Bhūṣakāya Namaḥ.
ॐ ह्रीं हेतिदाय नम:		Om Hrīm Hētidāya Namaḥ.
ॐ ह्रीं हेतिधर पूजिताय नम:		Om Hrīm Hētidhara Pūjitāya Namaḥ.
ॐ ह्रीं हंसाय नम:		Om Hrīm Hamsāya Namaḥ.
ॐ ह्रीं हंस गतयभ्राम:		Om Hrīm Hamsāgatayē Namaḥ.

ॐ ह्रीं हंस मन्त्र रूपाय नम:		Om Hrīm Hamsa Mantra Rūpāya Namaḥ.
ॐ ह्रीं हंसी पतयभ्राम:		Om Hrīm Hamsī Pataye Namaḥ.
ॐ ह्रीं हरोन्मत्ताय नम:	640	Om Hrīm Harōnmattāya Namaḥ.
ॐ ह्रीं हंसीशाय नम:		Om Hrīm Hamsīśāya Namaḥ.
ॐ ह्रीं हरवल्लभाय नम:		Om Hrīm Hara Vallabhāya Namaḥ.
ॐ ह्रीं हर पुष्प प्रभाय नम:		Om Hrīm Hara Puṣpa Prabhāya Namaḥ.
ॐ ह्रीं हंसी प्रियाय नम:		Om Hrīm Hamsī Priyāya Namaḥ.
ॐ ह्रीं हंस विलासिताय नम:		Om Hrīm Hamsavilāsitāya Namaḥ.
ॐ ह्रीं हरजीवरताय नम:		Om Hrīm Harajīvaratāya Namaḥ.
ॐ ह्रीं हारिन नम:		Om Hrīm Hārīṇē Namaḥ.
ॐ ह्रीं हरिताय नम:		Om Hrīm Haritāya Namaḥ.
ॐ ह्रीं हरिताम्पतय नम:		Om Hrīm Haritāmpatayē Namaḥ.
ॐ ह्रीं हरित्प्रभवभ्राम:	650	Om Hrīm Haritprabhavē Namaḥ.
ॐ ह्रीं हरित्पालाय नम:		Om Hrīm Haritpālāya Namaḥ.
ॐ ह्रीं हरिदन्तर नायकाय नम:		Om Hrīm Haridantara Nāyakāya Namaḥ.
ॐ ह्रीं हरिदीशाय नम:		Om Hrīm Haridīśāya Namaḥ.
ॐ ह्रीं हरित्राणाय नम:		Om Hrīm Haritprāṇāya Namaḥ.
ॐ ह्रीं हरिप्रिय प्रियाय नम:		Om Hrīm Hari Priya Priyāya Namaḥ.
ॐ ह्रीं हिताय नम:		Om Hrīm Hitāya Namaḥ.
ॐ ह्रीं हम्बम्बाय नम:		Om Hrīm Hērambāya Namaḥ.

ॐ ह्रीं हुङ्कृतिक्रुद्धाय नम: ।	Om Hrīm Huṅkru'ti Kruddhāya Namaḥ.
ॐ ह्रीं हेरम्बानन्दाय नम: ।	Om Hrīm Hērambānandāya Namaḥ.
ॐ ह्रीं हुङ्कृतय नम: । 660	Om Hrīm Huṅkru'tayē Namaḥ.
ॐ ह्रीं हरयभ्रम: ।	Om Hrīm Harayē Namaḥ.
ॐ ह्रीं हेरम्ब प्राणसंहर्त्रे नम: ।	Om Hrīm Hēramba Prāṇa Samhartrē Namaḥ.

ॐ ह्रीं हेरम्ब हृदय प्रियाय नम:		Om Hrīm Hēramba Hru'daya Priyāya Namaḥ.
ॐ ह्रीं क्षमा पतय नम:		Om Hrīm Kṣamāpatayē Namaḥ.
ॐ ह्रीं क्षणाय नम:		Om Hrīm Kṣaṇāya Namaḥ.
ॐ ह्रीं क्षान्ताय नम:		Om Hrīm Kṣāntāya Namaḥ.
ॐ ह्रीं क्षुरधाराय नम:		Om Hrīm Kṣuradhārāya Namaḥ.
ॐ ह्रीं क्षितीश्वराय नम:		Om Hrīm Kṣitīśvarāya Namaḥ.
ॐ ह्रीं क्षितीशाय नम:		Om Hrīm Kṣitīśāya Namaḥ.
ॐ ह्रीं क्षितिभृतभ्राम:	670	Om Hrīm Kṣitibhru'tē Namaḥ.
ॐ ह्रीं क्षीणाय नम:		Om Hrīm Kṣīṇāya Namaḥ.
ॐ ह्रीं क्षितिपालाय नम:		Om Hrīm Kṣitipālāya Namaḥ.
ॐ ह्रीं क्षितिप्रभव नम:		Om Hrīm Kṣitiprabhavē Namaḥ.
ॐ ह्रीं क्षितीशानाय नम:		Om Hrīm Kṣitīśānāya Namaḥ.
ॐ ह्रीं क्षितिप्राणाय नम:		Om Hrīm Kṣiti Prāṇāya Namaḥ.
ॐ ह्रीं क्षितिनायक सत्प्रियाय नम:		Om Hrīm Kṣitināyaka Satpriyāya Namaḥ.
ॐ ह्रीं क्षितिराजाय नम:		Om Hrīm Kṣitirājāya Namaḥ.
ॐ ह्रीं क्षणपतय नम:		Om Hrīm Kṣaṇapatayē Namaḥ.
ॐ ह्रीं क्षणश्वराय नम:	680	Om Hrīm Kṣaṇēśvarāya Namaḥ.
ॐ ह्रीं क्षणप्रियाय नम:		Om Hrīm Kṣaṇapriyāya Namaḥ.
ॐ ह्रीं क्षमानाथाय नम:		Om Hrīm Kṣamānāthāya Namaḥ.

ॐ ह्रीं क्षणदा नायक प्रियाय नम: ।	Om Hrīm Kṣaṇadā Nāyaka Priyāya Namaḥ.
ॐ ह्रीं क्षणिकाय नम: ।	Om Hrīm Kṣaṇikāya Namaḥ.
ॐ ह्रीं क्षणकाधीशाय नम: ।	Om Hrīm Kṣaṇakātī⁴Śāya Namaḥ.
ॐ ह्रीं क्षणदा प्राणदाय नम: ।	Om Hrīm Kṣaṇadā Prāṇadāya Namaḥ.
ॐ ह्रीं क्षमिनेभ्राम: ।	Om Hrīm Kṣamiṇē Namaḥ.
ॐ ह्रीं क्षमाय नम: ।	Om Hrīm Kṣamāya Namaḥ.
ॐ ह्रीं क्षोणीपतय नम: ।	Om Hrīm Kṣōṇīpatayē Namaḥ.
ॐ ह्रीं क्षोभाय नम: । 690	Om Hrīm Kṣōbhāya Namaḥ.
ॐ ह्रीं क्षोभकारिन नम: ।	Om Hrīm Kṣōbhakāriṇē Namaḥ.
ॐ ह्रीं क्षमाप्रियाय नम: ।	Om Hrīm Kṣamā Priyāya Namaḥ.
ॐ ह्रीं क्षमाशीलाय नम: ।	Om Hrīm Kṣamāśīlāya Namaḥ.
ॐ ह्रीं क्षमारूपाय नम: ।	Om Hrīm Kṣamārūpāya Namaḥ.
ॐ ह्रीं क्षमा मण्डल मण्डिताय नम: ।	Om Hrīm Kṣamā Maṇḍala Maṇḍitāya Namaḥ.
ॐ ह्रीं क्षमानाथाय नम: ।	Om Hrīm KṣamānāthāYa Namaḥ.
ॐ ह्रीं क्षमाधाराय नम: ।	Om Hrīm Kṣamādhārāya Namaḥ.
ॐ ह्रीं क्षमाधारिन नम: ।	Om Hrīm Kṣamādhāriṇē Namaḥ.
ॐ ह्रीं क्षमाधराय नम: ।	Om Hrīm Kṣamādharāya Namaḥ.
ॐ ह्रीं क्षम्र क्षीणरुजाक्षुद्राय नम: । 700	Om Hrīm Kṣēma Kṣīṇa Rujākṣudrāya Namaḥ. 700

ॐ हीं क्षुद्रपालविशारदाय नमः ।	Om Hrīm Kṣudrapāla Viśāradāya Namaḥ.
ॐ हीं क्षुद्रासनाय नमः ।	Om Hrīm Kṣudrāsanāya Namaḥ.
ॐ हीं क्षणाकाराय नमः ।	Om Hrīm Kṣaṇākārāya Namaḥ.
ॐ हीं क्षीरपानक तत्पराय नमः ।	Om Hrīm Kṣīrapānaka Tatparāya Namaḥ.
ॐ हीं क्षीरशायिनभ्रमः ।	Om Hrīm Kṣīraśāyiṉē Namaḥ.
ॐ हीं क्षणभ्रानाय नमः ।	Om Hrīm Kṣaṇēśānāya Namaḥ.
ॐ हीं क्षोणीभृव नमः ।	Om Hrīm Kṣōṇībhruvē Namaḥ.
ॐ हीं क्षणदोत्सवाय नमः ।	Om Hrīm Kṣaṇadōtsavāya Namaḥ.
ॐ हीं क्षभ्रङ्कराय नमः ।	Om Hrīm Kṣēmaṅkarāya Namaḥ.
ॐ हीं क्षमाळुब्धाय नमः । 710	Om Hrīm Kṣamāḷubdhāya Namaḥ. 710
ॐ हीं क्षमीश्वराय नमः ।	Om Hrīm Kṣamīśvarāya Namaḥ.
ॐ हीं क्षमाकामाय नमः ।	Om Hrīm Kṣamākāmāya Namaḥ.
ॐ हीं क्षमा सास्त्र विचारथाय नमः ।	Om Hrīm Kṣamā Sāstra Vicārathāya Namaḥ.
ॐ हीं क्षमा हृदय मण्डनाय नमः।	Om Hrīm Kṣamā Hru'daya Maṇḍanāya Namaḥ.
ॐ हीं नीलाद्रि रुचिरा वष्ब्राय नमः ।	Om Hrīm Nīlādri Rucirā Vēśāya Namaḥ.
ॐ हीं नीलोपर्वत सन्निभाय नमः ।	Om Hrīm Nīlōparvata Sannibhāya Namaḥ.
ॐ हीं नाल मणि प्रभारम्माय नमः ।	Om Hrīm Nāla Maṇi Prabhāramyāya Namaḥ.

ॐ ह्रीं नील भूषण भूषिताय नम: |	Om Hrīm Nīla Bhūṣaṇa Bhūṣitāya Namaḥ.
ॐ ह्रीं नीलवर्णाय नम: |	Om Hrīm Nīlavarṇāya Namaḥ.
ॐ ह्रीं नीलभ्रुवाय नम: | 720	Om Hrīm Nīlabhruvāya Namaḥ. 720
ॐ ह्रीं मुण्ड माला विभूषिताय नम: |	Om Hrīm Muṇḍa Mālā Vibhūṣitāya Namaḥ.
ॐ ह्रीं मुण्डस्थाय नम: |	Om Hrīm Muṇḍasthāya Namaḥ.
ॐ ह्रीं मुण्डसन्तुष्टाय नम: |	Om Hrīm Muṇḍa Santuṣṭāya Namaḥ.
ॐ ह्रीं मुण्ड माला धराय नम: |	Om Hrīm Muṇḍa Mālā Dharāya Namaḥ.
ॐ ह्रीं नयाय नम: |	Om Hrīm Nayāya Namaḥ.
ॐ ह्रीं दिग्वासाय नम: |	Om Hrīm Digvāsāya Namaḥ.
ॐ ह्रीं विदिताकाराय नम: |	Om Hrīm Viditākārāya Namaḥ.
ॐ ह्रीं दिगम्बर वर प्रदाय नम: |	Om Hrīm Digambara Vara Pradāya Namaḥ.
ॐ ह्रीं दिगम्बरीशाय नम: |	Om Hrīm Digambarīśāya Namaḥ.
ॐ ह्रीं आनन्दिनभ्राम: | 730	Om Hrīm Ānandiṉē Namaḥ.
ॐ ह्रीं दिग्बन्धनाय नम: |	Om Hrīm Digbandhāya Namaḥ.
ॐ ह्रीं प्रियनन्दनाय नम: |	Om Hrīm Priyanandanāya Namaḥ.
ॐ ह्रीं पिङ्गलैक जटाय नम: |	Om Hrīm Piṅgalaikajaṭāya Namaḥ.
ॐ ह्रीं हृष्टाय नम: |	Om Hrīm Hru'ṣṭāya Namaḥ.
ॐ ह्रीं डमरूवादन प्रियाय नम: |	Om Hrīm Ḍamarū Vādanapriyāya Namaḥ.
ॐ ह्रीं श्रेणीकराय नम: |	Om Hrīm Śrēṇīkarāya Namaḥ.

ॐ ह्रीं श्रेणीशाय नम:		Om Hrīm Śrēṇīśāya Namaḥ.
ॐ ह्रीं खड्गधृत नम:		Om Hrīm Khaḍgadhru'tē Namaḥ.
ॐ ह्रीं खड्गपालकाय नम:		Om Hrīm Khaḍgapālakāya Namaḥ.
ॐ ह्रीं शूलहस्ताय नम:	740	Om Hrīm Śūlahastāya Namaḥ.
ॐ ह्रीं मतङ्गाभाय नम:		Om Hrīm Mataṅgābhāya Namaḥ.
ॐ ह्रीं मातङ्गोत्सव सुन्दराय नम:		Om Hrīm Mātaṅgōtsava Sundarāya Namaḥ.
ॐ ह्रीं अभयङ्कराय नम:		Om Hrīm Abhayaṅkarāya Namaḥ.
ॐ ह्रीं ऊर्वङ्काय नम:		Om Hrīm Ūrvaṅkāya Namaḥ.
ॐ ह्रीं लङ्कापतिर्विनाशनाय नम:		Om Hrīm Laṅkāpati Vināśaṉāya Namaḥ.
ॐ ह्रीं विनायकाय नम:		Om Hrīm Vināyakāya Namaḥ.
ॐ ह्रीं नगेश्वयाय नम:		Om Hrīm Nagēśayāya Namaḥ.
ॐ ह्रीं नगेश्वानाय नम:		Om Hrīm Nagēśānāya Namaḥ.
ॐ ह्रीं नाग मण्डल मण्डिताय नम:		Om Hrīm Nāgamaṇḍala Maṇḍitāya Namaḥ.
ॐ ह्रीं नागाकाराय नम:	750	Om Hrīm Nāgākārāya Namaḥ.
ॐ ह्रीं नागधीशाय नम:		Om Hrīm Nāgadhīśāya Namaḥ.
ॐ ह्रीं नागशायिन नम:		Om Hrīm Nāgaśāyiṉē Namaḥ.
ॐ ह्रीं नगप्रियाय नम:		Om Hrīm Nagapriyāya Namaḥ.
ॐ ह्रीं घटोत्सवाय नम:		Om Hrīm Ghaṭōtsavāya Namaḥ.
ॐ ह्रीं घटाकाराय नम:		Om Hrīm Ghaṭākārāya Namaḥ.

ॐ ह्रीं घण्टावाद्याय शारदाय नम: ।	Om Hrīm Ghaṇṭāvāt³Ya Viśāradāya Namaḥ.
ॐ ह्रीं कपालपाणिन नम: ।	Om Hrīm Kapālapāṇiṇē Namaḥ.
ॐ ह्रीं अम्बश्राय नम: ।	Om Hrīm Ambēśāya Namaḥ.
ॐ ह्रीं कपालाशन शारदाय नम: ।	Om Hrīm Kapālāśana Śāradāya Namaḥ.
ॐ ह्रीं पद्मपाणये नम: । 760	Om Hrīm Padmapāṇayē Namaḥ. 760
ॐ ह्रीं करालास्याय नम: ।	Om Hrīm Karālāsya Namaḥ.
ॐ ह्रीं स्त्रिनत्राय नम: ।	Om Hrīm Strinētrāya Namaḥ.
ॐ ह्रीं नागवल्लभाय नम: ।	Om Hrīm Nāgavallabhāya Namaḥ.
ॐ ह्रीं किङ्किणी जाल संहृष्टाय नम: ।	Om Hrīm Kiṅkiṇī Jāla Samhru'ṣṭāya Namaḥ.
ॐ ह्रीं जनाशयाय नम: ।	Om Hrīm Janāśayāya Namaḥ.
ॐ ह्रीं जननायकाय नम: ।	Om Hrīm Jananāyakāya Namaḥ.
ॐ ह्रीं अपमृत्युहराय नम: ।	Om Hrīm Apamru'tyu Harāya Namaḥ.
ॐ ह्रीं मायामोह मूल विनाशकाय नम: ।	Om Hrīm Māyā Mōha Mūla Vināśakāya Namaḥ.
ॐ ह्रीं आयुकाय नम: ।	Om Hrīm Āyukāya Namaḥ.
ॐ ह्रीं कमलानाथाय नम: । 770	Om Hrīm Kamalānāthāya Namaḥ.
ॐ ह्रीं कमलाकान्त वल्लभाय नम: ।	Om Hrīm Kamalākānta Vallabhāya Namaḥ.
ॐ ह्रीं राज्यदाय नम: ।	Om Hrīm Rājyadāya Namaḥ.

ॐ ह्रीं राजराजश्राय नम: |	Om Hrīm Rājarājēśāya Namaḥ.
ॐ ह्रीं राजीवाय नम: |	Om Hrīm Rājīvāya Namaḥ.
ॐ ह्रीं शोभनाय नम: |	Om Hrīm Śōbhanāya Namaḥ.
ॐ ह्रीं डाकिनीनायकाय नम: |	Om Hrīm Ḍākinīnāyakāya Namaḥ.
ॐ ह्रीं नित्याय नम: |	Om Hrīm Nityāya Namaḥ.
ॐ ह्रीं नित्यधर्मपरायणाय नम: |	Om Hrīm Nityadharma Parāyaṇāya Namaḥ.
ॐ ह्रीं डाकिनीहृदयाय नम: |	Om Hrīm Ḍākinīhru'dayāya Namaḥ.
ॐ ह्रीं ज्ञानिन नम: | 780	Om Hrīm Jñāninē Namaḥ.
ॐ ह्रीं डाकिनी दह्ननायकाय नम: |	Om Hrīm Dākinīdēhanāyakāya Namaḥ.
ॐ ह्रीं डाकिनी प्राणदाय नम: |	Om Hrīm Ḍākinīprāṇadāya Namaḥ.
ॐ ह्रीं सिद्धाय नम: |	Om Hrīm Siddhāya Namaḥ.
ॐ ह्रीं श्रद्धश्र चरिताय नम: |	Om Hrīm Śraddhēya Caritāya Namaḥ.
ॐ ह्रीं विभव नम: |	Om Hrīm Vibhavē Namaḥ.
ॐ ह्रीं हझप्रभाय नम: |	Om Hrīm Hēmaprabhāya Namaḥ.
ॐ ह्रीं हिमझ्रानाय नम: |	Om Hrīm Himēśānāya Namaḥ.
ॐ ह्रीं हिमानी प्रिय दर्शनाय नम: |	Om Hrīm Himānī Priyadarśanāya Namaḥ.
ॐ ह्रीं हझ्रदाय नम: |	Om Hrīm Hēmadāya Namaḥ.
ॐ ह्रीं नर्मदाय नम: | 790	Om Hrīm Narmadāya Namaḥ.
ॐ ह्रीं मानिन नम: |	Om Hrīm Māṇinē Namaḥ.

ॐ ह्रीं नामधेयाय नम:		Om Hrīm Nāmadhēyāya Namaḥ.
ॐ ह्रीं नगात्मजाय नम:		Om Hrīm Nagātmajāya Namaḥ.
ॐ ह्रीं वैकुण्ठाय नम:		Om Hrīm Vaikuṇṭhāya Namaḥ.
ॐ ह्रीं वासुकि प्राणाय नम:		Om Hrīm Vāsukiprāṇāya Namaḥ.
ॐ ह्रीं वासुकी कण्ठ भूषणाय नम:		Om Hrīm Vāsukī Kaṇṭha Bhūṣaṇāya Namaḥ.
ॐ ह्रीं कुण्डलीशाय नम:		Om Hrīm Kuṇḍalīśāya Namaḥ.
ॐ ह्रीं मुखध्वंसिन नम:		Om Hrīm Mugadhvamsiṉē Namaḥ.
ॐ ह्रीं मखराजाय नम:		Om Hrīm Magarājāya Namaḥ.
ॐ ह्रीं मखाकाराय नम:	800	Om Hrīm Magākārāya Namaḥ.
ॐ ह्रीं मखेश्वराय नम:		Om Hrīm Makhēśvarāya Namaḥ.
ॐ ह्रीं मखाकाराय नम:		Om Hrīm Makhākārāya Namaḥ.
ॐ ह्रीं मखाधीशाय नम:		Om Hrīm Makhādhīśāya Namaḥ.
ॐ ह्रीं मखमालि विभूषणाय नम:		Om Hrīm Makhamāli Vibhūṣaṇāya Namaḥ.
ॐ ह्रीं अम्बिका वल्लभाय नम:		Om Hrīm Ambikā Vallabhāya Namaḥ.
ॐ ह्रीं वाणीमतिर्विशारदाय नम:		Om Hrīm Vāṇīmatayēvāṇī Viśāradāya Namaḥ.
ॐ ह्रीं वाणीशाय नम:		Om Hrīm Vāṇīśāya Namaḥ.
ॐ ह्रीं वचन प्राणाय नम:		Om Hrīm Vacana Prāṇāya Namaḥ.
ॐ ह्रीं वचनस्थाय नम:		Om Hrīm Vacanasthāya Namaḥ.
ॐ ह्रीं वनप्रियाय नम:	810	Om Hrīm Vanapriyāya Namaḥ.

ॐ ह्रीं वेलाधाराय नम: ।	Om Hrīm Vēlādhārāya Namaḥ.
ॐ ह्रीं दिशामीशाय नम: ।	Om Hrīm Diśāmīśāya Namaḥ.
ॐ ह्रीं दिग्भागाय नम: ।	Om Hrīm Digbhāgāya Namaḥ.
ॐ ह्रीं दिगीश्वराय नम: ।	Om Hrīm Digīśvarāya Namaḥ.
ॐ ह्रीं दुराराध्याय नम: ।	Om Hrīm Durārādhyāya Namaḥ.
ॐ ह्रीं दारिद्र्य भञ्जनाय नम: ।	Om Hrīm Dāridrya Bhañjaṉāya Namaḥ.
ॐ ह्रीं तर्क प्रियाय नम: ।	Om Hrīm Tarka Priyāya Namaḥ.
ॐ ह्रीं तर्क्याय नम: ।	Om Hrīm Tarkyāya Namaḥ.
ॐ ह्रीं वित्तर्क्याय नम: ।	Om Hrīm Vittarkyāya Namaḥ.
ॐ ह्रीं तर्क वल्लभाय नम: । 820	Om Hrīm Tarka Vallabhāya Namaḥ. 820
ॐ ह्रीं तर्कसिद्धाय नम: ।	Om Hrīm Tarkasiddhāya Namaḥ.
ॐ ह्रीं सुसिद्धात्मन नम: ।	Om Hrīm Susiddhātmaṉē Namaḥ.
ॐ ह्रीं सिद्धदेहाय नम: ।	Om Hrīm Siddhadēhāya Namaḥ.
ॐ ह्रीं ग्रहासनाय नम: ।	Om Hrīm Grahāsanāya Namaḥ.
ॐ ह्रीं ग्रहगर्वाय नम: ।	Om Hrīm Grahagarvāya Namaḥ.
ॐ ह्रीं ग्रहेशानाय नम: ।	Om Hrīm Grahēśānāya Namaḥ.
ॐ ह्रीं गन्धाय नम: ।	Om Hrīm Gandhāya Namaḥ.
ॐ ह्रीं गन्धिन नम: ।	Om Hrīm Gantiṉē Namaḥ.
ॐ ह्रीं विशारदाय नम: ।	Om Hrīm Vēlāradāya Namaḥ.
ॐ ह्रीं मङ्गळाय नम: । 830	Om Hrīm Maṅgaḷāya Namaḥ.
ॐ ह्रीं मङ्गळा काराय नम: ।	Om Hrīm Maṅgaḷākārāya Namaḥ.

ॐ ह्रीं मङ्गळ वाद्य वादकाय नम: ।	Om Hrīm Maṅgaḷa Vādya Vādakāya Namaḥ.
ॐ ह्रीं मङ्गळीशाय नम: ।	Om Hrīm Maṅgaḷīśāya Namaḥ.
ॐ ह्रीं विमानस्थाय नम: ।	Om Hrīm Vimānasthāya Namaḥ.
ॐ ह्रीं विमानैकाय नम: ।	Om Hrīm Vimānaikāya Namaḥ.
ॐ ह्रीं सुनायकाय नम: ।	Om Hrīm Sunāyakāya Namaḥ.
ॐ ह्रीं बुधेश्राय नम: ।	Om Hrīm Budhēśāya Namaḥ.
ॐ ह्रीं विविधा धीशाय नम: ।	Om Hrīm Vividhā Dhīśāya Namaḥ.
ॐ ह्रीं बुधवाराय नम: ।	Om Hrīm Budhavārāya Namaḥ.
ॐ ह्रीं बुधाकराय नम: । 840	Om Hrīm Budhākarāya Namaḥ.
ॐ ह्रीं बुधनाथाय नम: ।	Om Hrīm Budhanāthāya Namaḥ.
ॐ ह्रीं बुध प्रीताय नम: ।	Om Hrīm Budha Prītāya Namaḥ.
ॐ ह्रीं बुध वन्द्याय नम: ।	Om Hrīm Budhavandyāya Namaḥ.
ॐ ह्रीं बुधाधिपाय नम: ।	Om Hrīm Budhādhipāya Namaḥ.
ॐ ह्रीं बुध सिद्धाय नम: ।	Om Hrīm Budhasiddhāya Namaḥ.
ॐ ह्रीं बुध प्राणाय नम: ।	Om Hrīm Budhaprāṇāya Namaḥ.
ॐ ह्रीं बुधप्रियाय नम: ।	Om Hrīm Budha Priyāya Namaḥ.
ॐ ह्रीं बुधाय नम: ।	Om Hrīm Budhāya Namaḥ.
ॐ ह्रीं बुद्धाय नम: ।	Om Hrīm Buddhāya Namaḥ.
ॐ ह्रीं सोमाय नम: । 850	Om Hrīm Sōmāya Namaḥ. 850
ॐ ह्रीं सोमसमाकाराय नम: ।	Om Hrīm Sōmasamākārāya Namaḥ.

ॐ ह्रीं सोमपाय नम: |	Om Hrīm Sōmapāya Namaḥ.
ॐ ह्रीं सोमनायकाय नम: |	Om Hrīm Sōmanāyakāya Namaḥ.
ॐ ह्रीं सोमप्रभाय नम: |	Om Hrīm Sōmaprabhāya Namaḥ.
ॐ ह्रीं सोमसिद्धाय नम: |	Om Hrīm Sōmasiddhāya Namaḥ.
ॐ ह्रीं सोमेश्वराय नम: |	Om Hrīm Sōmēśvarāya Namaḥ.
ॐ ह्रीं मनोरूपाय नम: |	Om Hrīm Maṉō Rūpāya Namaḥ.
ॐ ह्रीं प्राणरूपाय नम: |	Om Hrīm Prāṇa Rūpāya Namaḥ.
ॐ ह्रीं प्रणकाय नम: |	Om Hrīm Praṇākāya Namaḥ.
ॐ ह्रीं कामदाय नम: | 860	Om Hrīm Kāmadāya Namaḥ.
ॐ ह्रीं कामग्न नम: |	Om Hrīm Kāmagṉē Namaḥ.
ॐ ह्रीं बौद्ध कामनाफलदाय नम: |	Om Hrīm Bauddhakāmanā Phaladāya Namaḥ.
ॐ ह्रीं अधिरूपाय नम: |	Om Hrīm Adhi Rūpāya Namaḥ.
ॐ ह्रीं त्रिदशाय नम: |	Om Hrim Tridaśāya Namaḥ.
ॐ ह्रीं दशरात्रीशाय नम: |	Om Hrīm Daśarātrīśāya Namaḥ.
ॐ ह्रीं दशानन विनाशकाय नम: |	Om Hrīm Daśānana Vināśakāya Namaḥ.
ॐ ह्रीं लक्ष्मणाय नम: |	Om Hrīm Lakṣmaṇāya Namaḥ.
ॐ ह्रीं लक्षसम्भर्त्राय नम: |	Om Hrīm Lakṣasambhartrāya Namaḥ.
ॐ ह्रीं लक्ष्यसङ्ख्याय नम: |	Om Hrīm Lakṣya Saṅkhyāya Namaḥ.
ॐ ह्रीं मन प्रियाय नम: | 870	Om Hrīm Mana Priyāya Namaḥ.
ॐ ह्रीं विभावसवे नम: |	Om Hrīm Vibhāvasavē Namaḥ.
ॐ ह्रीं नवेश्रनाय नम: |	Om Hrīm Navēśānāya Namaḥ.

ॐ ह्रीं त्रिलोक नायकाय नम:		Om Hrīm Trilōka Nāyakāya Namaḥ.
ॐ ह्रीं नगर प्रियाय नम:		Om Hrīm Nagarap Riyāya Namaḥ.
ॐ ह्रीं नरकान्तयभ्राम:		Om Hrīm Narakāntakāya Namaḥ.
ॐ ह्रीं नलोत्साहाय नम:		Om Hrīm Nalōtsāhāya Namaḥ.
ॐ ह्रीं नरदेव्याय नम:		Om Hrīm Naradēvāya Namaḥ.
ॐ ह्रीं नलाकृतयभ्राम:		Om Hrīm Nalākru'tayē Namaḥ.
ॐ ह्रीं नरपतयभ्राम:		Om Hrīm Narapatayē Namaḥ.
ॐ ह्रीं नरेशानाय नम:	880	Om Hrīm Narēśānāya Namaḥ.
ॐ ह्रीं नारायणाय नम:		Om Hrīm Nārāyaṇāya Namaḥ.
ॐ ह्रीं नरेश्वराय नम:		Om Hrīm Narēśvarāya Namaḥ.
ॐ ह्रीं अनिलाय नम:		Om Hrīm Anilāya Namaḥ.
ॐ ह्रीं मारुताय नम:		Om Hrīm Mārutāya Namaḥ.
ॐ ह्रीं मांसाय नम:		Om Hrīm Māmsāya Namaḥ.
ॐ ह्रीं मांसैकरस सञ्जिताय नम:		Om Hrīm Māmsaikarasa Sēvitāya Namaḥ.
ॐ ह्रीं मरीचयभ्राम:		Om Hrīm Marīcayē Namaḥ.
ॐ ह्रीं अमरेशानाय नम:		Om Hrīm Amarēśānāya Namaḥ.
ॐ ह्रीं मागधाय नम:		Om Hrīm Māgadhāya Namaḥ.
ॐ ह्रीं मगधप्रभव नम:	890	Om Hrīm Magadhaprabhavē Namaḥ. 890
ॐ ह्रीं सुन्दरी सञ्जकाय नम:		Om Hrīm Sundarī Sēvakāya Namaḥ.
ॐ ह्रीं द्वारिन नम:		Om Hrīm Dvāriṇē Namaḥ.

ॐ ह्रीं द्वारदेश निवासनाय नम:		Om Hrīm Dvāradēśa Nivāsanāya Namaḥ.
ॐ ह्रीं देवकी गर्भ सञ्जाताय नम:		Om Hrīm Dēvakī Garbhasañjātāya Namaḥ.
ॐ ह्रीं देवकी सेवकाय नम:		Om Hrīm Dēvakīsēvakāya Namaḥ.
ॐ ह्रीं कुहुव नम:		Om Hrīm Kuhuvē Namaḥ.
ॐ ह्रीं बृहस्पतय नम:		Om Hrīm Bru'haspatayē Namaḥ.
ॐ ह्रीं कवय नम:		Om Hrīm Kavayē Namaḥ.
ॐ ह्रीं शुक्राय नम:		Om Hrīm Śukrāya Namaḥ.
ॐ ह्रीं शारदासाधन प्रियाय नम:	900	Om Hrīm Śāradāsāthana Priyāya Namaḥ. 900
ॐ ह्रीं शारदा साधक प्राणाय नम:		Om Hrīm Śāradā Sādhaka Prāṇāya Namaḥ.
ॐ ह्रीं शारदा सेवकोत्सुकाय नम:		Om Hrīm Śāradā Sēvakōtsukāya Namaḥ.
ॐ ह्रीं शारदा साधक श्रेष्ठाय नम:		Om Hrīm Śāradā Sādhaka Śrēṣṭāya Namaḥ.
ॐ ह्रीं मधुपानसदारतय: नम:		Om Hrīm Madhupānasa Dāratayē Namaḥ.
ॐ ह्रीं गजप्रभव नम:		Om Hrīm Kajaprabhavē Namaḥ.
ॐ ह्रीं मोदकादान सम्प्रीताय नम:		Om Hrīm Mōdakādāna Samprītāya Namaḥ.
ॐ ह्रीं मोदकामोदाय नम:		Om Hrīm Mōdakāmōdāya Namaḥ.
ॐ ह्रीं मोदिताय नम:		Om Hrīm Mōditāya Namaḥ.
ॐ ह्रीं आमोदिदाय नम:		Om Hrīm Āmōditāya Namaḥ.

ॐ ह्रीं आनन्दाय नम:	910	*Om Hrīm Ānandanāya Namaḥ. 910*
ॐ ह्रीं नन्दाय नम:		*Om Hrīm Nandāya Namaḥ.*
ॐ ह्रीं नन्दिकेश्वाय नम:		*Om Hrīm Nandikēśāya Namaḥ.*
ॐ ह्रीं महेश्वराय नम:		*Om Hrīm Mahēśvarāya Namaḥ.*
ॐ ह्रीं नन्दिप्रियाय नम:		*Om Hrīm Nandi Priyāya Namaḥ.*
ॐ ह्रीं नदीनाथाय नम:		*Om Hrīm Nadīnāthāya Namaḥ.*
ॐ ह्रीं नदीतीरतरुस्तथाय नम:		*Om Hrīm Nadītīratarustathāya Namaḥ.*
ॐ ह्रीं तपनाय नम:		*Om Hrīm Tapanāya Namaḥ.*
ॐ ह्रीं तापनाय नम:		*Om Hrīm Tāpanāya Namaḥ.*
ॐ ह्रीं तप्त्र नम:		*Om Hrīm Taptrē Namaḥ.*
ॐ ह्रीं तापहाय नम:	920	*Om Hrīm Tāpahāya Namaḥ. 920*
ॐ ह्रीं तापकारकाय नम:		*Om Hrīm Tāpakārakāya Namaḥ.*
ॐ ह्रीं पतङ्गाय नम:		*Om Hrīm Pataṅgāya Namaḥ.*
ॐ ह्रीं गोमुखाय नम:		*Om Hrīm Gōmukhāya Namaḥ.*
ॐ ह्रीं गौराय नम:		*Om Hrīm Gaurāya Namaḥ.*
ॐ ह्रीं गोपालाय नम:		*Om Hrīm Gōpālāya Namaḥ.*
ॐ ह्रीं गोपवर्धनाय नम:		*Om Hrīm Gōpavardhanāya Namaḥ.*
ॐ ह्रीं गोपतयभ्रम:		*Om Hrīm Gōpatayē Namaḥ.*
ॐ ह्रीं गोपसंहत्रे नम:		*Om Hrīm Gōpasamhartrē Namaḥ.*
ॐ ह्रीं गोविन्दैक प्रियाय नम:		*Om Hrīm Gōvindaika Priyāya Namaḥ.*
ॐ ह्रीं अतिगाय नम:	930	*Om Hrīm Atigāya Namaḥ. 930*

ॐ ह्रीं गव्येष्ठाय नम: ।	Om Hrīm Gavyēṣṭhāya Namaḥ.
ॐ ह्रीं गणरम्भाय नम: ।	Om Hrīm Gaṇarambhāya Namaḥ.
ॐ ह्रीं गुणसिन्धव नम: ।	Om Hrīm Guṇa Sindhavē Namaḥ.
ॐ ह्रीं गुणा प्रियाय नम: ।	Om Hrīm Guṇā Priyāya Namaḥ.
ॐ ह्रीं गुणपूज्याय नम: ।	Om Hrīm Guṇa Pūjyāya Namaḥ.
ॐ ह्रीं गुणोपेब्राय नम: ।	Om Hrīm Guṇōpētāya Namaḥ.
ॐ ह्रीं गुणवाद्याय नम: ।	Om Hrīm Guṇavādyāya Namaḥ.
ॐ ह्रीं गुणोत्सवाय नम: ।	Om Hrīm Guṇōtsavāya Namaḥ.
ॐ ह्रीं गुणिणे नम: ।	Om Hrīm Guṇiṇē Namaḥ.
ॐ ह्रीं कञ्चलाय नम: । 940	Om Hrīm Kēvalāya Namaḥ. 940
ॐ ह्रीं गर्भाय नम: ।	Om Hrīm Garbhāya Namaḥ.
ॐ ह्रीं सुगर्भाय नम: ।	Om Hrīm Sugarbhāya Namaḥ.
ॐ ह्रीं गर्भरक्षकाय नम: ।	Om Hrīm Garbharakṣakāya Namaḥ.
ॐ ह्रीं गम्भीराय नम: ।	Om Hrīm Gambhīrāya Namaḥ.
ॐ ह्रीं धारकाय नम: ।	Om Hrīm Dhārakāya Namaḥ.
ॐ ह्रीं धर्त्रे नम: ।	Om Hrīm Dhartrē Namaḥ.
ॐ ह्रीं विधर्त्रे नम: ।	Om Hrīm Vidhartrē Namaḥ.
ॐ ह्रीं धर्मपालकाय नम: ।	Om Hrīm Dharmapālakāya Namaḥ.
ॐ ह्रीं जगदीशाय नम: ।	Om Hrīm Jagadīśāya Namaḥ.
ॐ ह्रीं जगन्मित्राय नम: । 950	Om Hrīm Jaganmitrāya Namaḥ. 950
ॐ ह्रीं जगज्जाड्य विनाशनाय नम: ।	Om Hrīm Jagajjāḍya Vināśanāya Namaḥ.

ॐ ह्रीं जगत्कर्त्रे नम: ।	Om Hrīm Jagatkartrē Namaḥ.
ॐ ह्रीं जगद्धात्रे नम: ।	Om Hrīm Jagaddhātrē Namaḥ.
ॐ ह्रीं जगत्प्रभवभ्राम: ।	Om Hrīm Jagad Prabhavē Namaḥ.
ॐ ह्रीं जगन्नादाय नम: ।	Om Hrīm Jagan Nādāya Namaḥ.
ॐ ह्रीं जगत्भोक्ताय नम: ।	Om Hrīm Jagad Bhōktāya Namaḥ.
ॐ ह्रीं जगज्जीवनाय नम: ।	Om Hrīm Jagaj Jīvanāya Namaḥ.
ॐ ह्रीं जीनानाय नम: ।	Om Hrīm Jīnānāya Namaḥ.
ॐ ह्रीं मालति पुष्प सम्प्रीताय नम: ।	Om Hrīm Mālati Puṣpa Samprītāya Namaḥ.
ॐ ह्रीं मालती कुसुमोत्सवाय नम: । 960	Om Hrīm Mālatī Kusu Mōtsavāya Namaḥ. 960
ॐ ह्रीं मालती कुसुमाकाराय नम: ।	Om Hrīm Mālatī Kusumākārāya Namaḥ.
ॐ ह्रीं मालती कुसुम प्रभव नम: ।	Om Hrīm Mālatī Kusuma Prabhavē Namaḥ.
ॐ ह्रीं रसाल मञ्जरी रम्याय नम: ।	Om Hrīm Rasāla Mañjarī Ramyāya Namaḥ.
ॐ ह्रीं रसाल गन्ध सेक्षिताय नम: ।	Om Hrīm Rasāla Gandha Sēvitāya Namaḥ.
ॐ ह्रीं रसालमञ्जरी लुब्धाय नम: ।	Om Hrīm Rasālamañjarī Lubdhāya Namaḥ.
ॐ ह्रीं रसाल तरु वल्लभाय नम: ।	Om Hrīm Rasāla Taruvallabhāya Namaḥ.
ॐ ह्रीं रसाल पादपासीनाय	Om Hrīm Rasāla Pādapāsīnāya Namaḥ.

नम:		
ॐ ह्रीं रसाल फल सुन्दराय नम:		Om Hrīm Rasāla Phala Sundarāya Namaḥ.
ॐ ह्रीं रसाल रस सन्तुष्टाय नम:		Om Hrīm Rasāla Rasa Santuṣṭāya Namaḥ.
ॐ ह्रीं रसाल रस सालयाय नम:	970	Om Hrīm Rasāla Rasa Sālayāya Namaḥ. 970
ॐ ह्रीं केतकी प्राण नाशकाय नम:		Om Hrīm Kētakī Prāṇa Nāśakāya Namaḥ.
ॐ ह्रीं केतकी पुष्प सन्तुष्टाय नम:		Om Hrīm Kētakī Puṣpa Santuṣṭāya Namaḥ.
ॐ ह्रीं केतकी गर्भ सम्भवाय नम:		Om Hrīm Kētakī Garbha Sambhavāya Namaḥ.
ॐ ह्रीं केतकी पत्र सङ्काशाय नम:		Om Hrīm Kētakī Patra Saṅkāśāya Namaḥ.
ॐ ह्रीं गर्तस्थाय नम:		Om Hrīm Gartasthāya Namaḥ.
ॐ ह्रीं गर्त गम्भीराय नम:		Om Hrīm Garta Gambhīrāya Namaḥ.
ॐ ह्रीं गर्ततीर निवासनाय नम:		Om Hrīm Garta Tīra Nivāsanāya Namaḥ.
ॐ ह्रीं गणसेव्याय नम:		Om Hrīm Gaṇasēvyāya Namaḥ.
ॐ ह्रीं गणाध्यक्षाय नम:		Om Hrīm Gaṇādhyakṣāya Namaḥ.
ॐ ह्रीं गणराजाय नम:	980	Om Hrīm Gaṇarājāya Namaḥ.
ॐ ह्रीं गणाह्वयाय नम:		Om Hrīm Gaṇāhvyāya Namaḥ.
ॐ ह्रीं आनन्द भैरवाय नम:		Om Hrīm Ānanda Bhairavāya Namaḥ.

ॐ ह्रीं भीरुभैरवाय नम: ।	Om Hrīm Bhīru Bhairavāya Namaḥ.
ॐ ह्रीं रुरुभैरवाय नम: ।	Om Hrīm Rurur Bhairavāya Namaḥ.
ॐ ह्रीं बगाय नम: ।	Om Hrīm Bagāya Namaḥ.
ॐ ह्रीं सुब्रह्म्य भैरवाय नम: ।	Om Hrīm Subrahmya Bhairavāya Namaḥ.

ॐ ह्रीं नामभैरवाय नम:		Om Hrīm Nāma Bhairavāya Namaḥ.
ॐ ह्रीं भूत भावनाय नम:		Om Hrīm Bhūta Bhāvanāya Namaḥ.
ॐ ह्रीं भैरवी तनयाय नम:		Om Hrīm Bhairavī Tanayāya Namaḥ.
ॐ ह्रीं देवी पुत्राय नम:	990	Om Hrīm Dēvī Putrāya Namaḥ.
ॐ ह्रीं पर्वत सन्निभाय नम:		Om Hrīm Parvata Sannibhāya Namaḥ.
ॐ ह्रीं श्रीभैरवाय नम:		Om Hrīm Śrī Bhairavāya Namaḥ.
ॐ ह्रीं मांसप्रियाय नम:		Om Hrīm Māmsa Priyāya Namaḥ.
ॐ ह्रीं मधुप्राणाय नम:		Om Hrīm Madhu Prāṇāya Namaḥ.
ॐ ह्रीं मधुमांस महोत्सवाय नम:		Om Hrīm Madhumāmsa Mahōtsavāya Namaḥ.
ॐ ह्रीं मधुपाय नम:		Om Hrīm Madhupāya Namaḥ.
ॐ ह्रीं मधुप सत्रष्ठाय नम:		Om Hrīm Madhupa Srēṣṭāya Namaḥ.
ॐ ह्रीं मधुपान सदारताय नम:		Om Hrīm Madhupāṉa Sadāratāya Namaḥ.
ॐ ह्रीं शुक्ल ज्योतिषे नम:		Om Hrīm Śukla Jyōtiṣē Namaḥ.
ॐ ह्रीं सहस्र दळ मद्यस्थाय नम:	1000	Om Hrīm Sahasra Daḷa Madyasthāya Namaḥ.

Thus ends the glorious 1000
names of Lord *Bhairava*.

*****

Śrī Bhairava Sahasranāma Stotram
श्रीभैरवसहस्रनामस्तोत्रम् ॥

दक्षउवाच –

दक्षज्ञ भक्तिसुलभ दक्षनायकवन्दित ।
भक्तानां काम्यसिद्ध्यर्थं निदानं ब्रूहि तत्त्वतः ॥ १

विनैव न्यासजालज्ञ पूजनज्ञ विना भवज्ञ ।
विनाऽपि कायक्लञ्जज्ञ विना जप्यज्ञ चञ्चर ॥ २

श्रीमहादज्ञ उवाच –

अस्य श्रीभैरव सहस्रनाम माला मन्त्रस्य ब्रह्मानन्द भैरव ऋषिः
अनुष्टुप्छन्दः बटुकभैरवो दक्षता ।
वं बीजं ह्रीं शक्तिः अभीष्टफलसिद्ध्यर्थे जपज्ञविनियोगः ॥

बटुकः कामदो नाथोऽनाथप्रियः प्रभाकरः ।
भैरवो भीतिहा दर्पः कन्दर्पो मीनकज्ञनः ॥ ३

रुद्रो वटुर्विभूतीशो भूतनाथः प्रजापतिः ।
दयालुः क्रूर ईशानो जनीशो लोकवल्लभः ॥ ४

दक्षो दैत्यज्ञरो वीरोवीरवन्द्यो दिवाकरः ।
बलिप्रियः सुरश्रेज्ञः कनिष्ठः कनिष्ठशिशुः ॥ ५

महाबलो महातज्ञा वित्तजित् द्युतिवर्धनः ।
तज्ञस्वी वीर्यवान्वृद्धो विवृद्धो भूतनायकः ॥ ६

कालः कपालकामादिविकारः काममर्दनः ।
कामिकारमणः कामी नायकः कालिकाप्रियः ॥ ७

कालीशः कामिनीकान्तः कालिकानन्दवर्धनः ।
कालिकाहृदयज्ञानी कालिकातनयो नयः ॥ ८

खगभ्रः खब्भ्रः खड्ग्रो विशिष्टः खड्गकप्रियः ।
कुमारः क्रोधनः कालाप्रियः पर्वतरक्षकः ॥ ९

गणभ्रयो गणनो गूढो गूढाशयो गणभ्रः ।
गणनाथो गणश्रष्ठो गणमुख्यो गणप्रियः ॥ १०

घोरनाथो घनश्यामो घनमूर्तिर्घनात्मकः ।
घोरनाशो घनभ्रानो धनपतिर्धनात्मकः ॥ ११

चम्पकाभाश्चिरञ्जीवो चारुवभ्रश्वराचरः ।
अन्त्योऽचिन्त्यगणो धीमान्सुचित्तस्थश्चितीश्वरः ॥ १२

छत्री छत्रपतिश्छत्रछिन्ननासामनः प्रियः ।
छिन्नाभश्छिन्नसन्तापश्छर्दिराच्छर्दनन्दनः ॥ १३

जनो जिष्णुर्जटीशानो जनार्दनो जनभ्रः ।
जनौको जनसन्तोषो जनजाड्य विनाशनः ॥ १४

जनप्रस्थो जनाराध्यो जनाध्यक्षो जनप्रियः ।
जीवहा जीवदो जन्तुर्जीविनाथो जनभ्रः ॥ १५

जयदो जित्वरो जिष्णुर्जयश्रीः जयवर्धनः ।
जयाभूमि जयाकारो जयहन्नुर्जयभ्रः ॥ १६

झङ्कारह्रदवान्तात्मा झङ्कारहन्नुरात्मभूः ।
ञभैश्वरी हरिर्भर्ता विभर्ता भृत्यकक्ष्वरः ॥ १७

ठीकारह्रदयोआत्म ठङ्क्ष्राष्टकनायकः ।
ठकारभूष्टरन्ध्रभ्राष्टिरीशाष्ठकुरपतिः ॥ १८

डुडीडक्काप्रियः पान्थो डुण्ढिराजो निरन्तकः ।
ताम्रस्तमीश्वरस्रोता तीर्थजातस्तडित्प्रभुः ॥ १९

ऋक्षरः ऋक्षकस्तभस्तार्क्ष्यकस्तम्भदभ्रः ।
स्थलजः स्थावरस्स्थाता स्थिरबुद्धिः स्थितन्द्रियः ॥ २०

स्थिरज्ञातिः स्थिरप्रीतिः स्थिरस्थितिः स्थिराशयः ।
दरो दामोदरो दम्भो दाडिमी कुसुमप्रियः ॥ २१

दरिद्रहादिमी दिव्यो दिव्यदह्लो दिवप्रभः ।
दीक्षाकारो दिवानाथो दिवसह्रो दिवाकरः ॥ २२

दीर्घशान्तिर्दलज्योतिर्दलह्लो दलसुन्दरः ।
दलप्रियो दलाभाशो दलश्रह्लो दलप्रभुः ॥ २३

दलकान्तिर्दलाकारो दलसह्रो दलार्चितः ।
दीर्घबाहुर्दलश्रह्लो दललूध्वदलाकृतिः ॥ २४

दानवह्रो दयासिन्धुर्दयालुर्दीनवल्लभः ।
धनह्रो धनदो धर्मो धनराजो धनप्रियः ॥ २५

धनप्रदो धनाध्यक्षो धनमान्यो धनञ्जयः ।
धीवरो धातुको धाता धूम्रो धूमच्छविवर्धनः ॥ २६

धनिष्ठो धनलच्छत्री धनकाम्यो धनह्वरः ।
धीरो धीरतरो धह्मूर्धीरह्लो धरणीप्रभूः ॥ २७

धरानाथो धराधीशो धरणीनायको धरः ।
धराकान्तो धरापालो धरणीभृद्धरात्रियः ॥ २८

धराधारो धराधृष्णो धृतराष्ट्रो धनीश्वरः ।
नारदो नरदो नह्वा नतिपूज्यो नतिप्रभूः ॥ २९

नतिलभ्यो नतीशानो नतिलघ्वो नतीश्वरः ।
पाण्डवः पार्थसम्पूज्यः पाथोदः प्रणतः पृथुः ॥ ३०

पुराणः प्राणदो पान्थो पाञ्चाली पावकप्रभुः ।
पृथिवीशः पृथासूनुः पृथिवी भृत्यकह्वरः ॥ ३१

पूर्वशूरपतिः श्रह्मान् प्रीतिदः प्रीतिवर्धनः ।
पार्वतीशः परह्मानः पार्वतीहृदयप्रियः ॥ ३२

पार्वतीरमणः पूतः पवित्रः पापनाशनः ।
पात्रीपात्रालिसन्तुष्टः परितुष्टः पुमान्प्रियः ॥ ३३

पर्वेशः पर्वताधीशः पर्वतो नायकात्मजः ।
फाल्गुनः फल्गुनो नाथः फणभ्रः फणिरक्षकः ॥ ३४

फणीपतिः फणीशानः फणालिन्दः फणाकृतिः ।
बलभद्रो बली बालो बलधीर्बलवर्धनः ॥ ३५

बलप्राणो बलाधीशो बलिदान प्रियङ्करः ।
बलिराजो बलिप्राणो बलिनाथो बलिप्रभुः ॥ ३६

बली बलश्च बालभ्रो बालकः प्रियदर्शनः ।
भद्री भद्रप्रदो भीमो भीमसभ्रो भयङ्करः ॥ ३७

भव्यो भव्यप्रियो भूतपतिर्भूतविनाशकः ।
भूतभ्रो भूतिदो भर्गो भूतभव्यो भवश्वरः ॥ ३८

भवानीशो भवभ्रानो भवानीनायको भवः ।
मकारो माधवो मानी मीनकक्षुर्महभ्ररः ॥ ३९

महर्षिर्मदनो मन्थो मिथुनभ्रोऽमराधिपः ।
मरीचिर्मजुलो मोहो मोहहा मोहमर्दनः ॥ ४०

मोहको मोहनो मभ्राप्रियो मोहविनाशकः ।
महीपतिर्महभ्रानो महाराजो महश्वरः ॥ ४१

महीश्वरो महीपालो महीनाथो महीप्रियः ।
महीधरो महीशानो मधुराजो मुनिप्रियः ॥ ४२

मौनी मौनधरो मभ्रो मन्दारो मतिवर्धनः ।
मतिदो मन्धरो मन्त्रो मन्त्रीशो मन्त्रनायकः ॥ ४३

मभ्रावी मानदो मानी मानहा मानमर्दनः ।
मीनगो मकराधीशो मकरो मणिरञ्जितः ॥ ४४

मणिरम्यो मणिभ्राता मणिमण्डल मण्डितः ।
मन्त्रिणो मन्त्रदो मुग्धो मोक्षदो मोक्षवल्लभः ॥ ४५

मल्लो मल्लप्रियो मन्त्रो मन्त्रको मन्त्रनप्रभः ।
मल्लिकागन्धरमणो मालतीकुसुमप्रभः ॥ ४६

मालतीशो मघाधीशो माघमूर्तिर्मघेश्वरः ।
मूलाभो मूलहा मूलो मूलदो मूलसम्भवः ॥ ४७

माणिक्यरोचिः सम्मुग्धो मणिकूटो मणिप्रियः ।
मुकुन्दो मदनो मन्दो मदवन्द्यो मनुप्रभुः ॥ ४८

मनस्स्थो मन्त्रकाधीशो मन्त्रका प्रियदर्शनः ।
यमोऽपि यामलो यज्ञा यादवो यदुनायकः ॥ ४९

याचको यज्ञको यज्ञो यज्ञेश्रो यज्ञवर्धनः ।
रमापती रमाधीशो रमेश्रो रामवल्लभः ॥ ५०

रमापती रमानाथो रमाकान्तो रमेश्वरः ।
रक्षती रमणो रामो रामेश्रो रामनन्दनः ॥ ५१

रम्यमूर्ती रतीशानो राकाया नायको रविः ।
लक्ष्मीधरो ललज्जिह्वो लक्ष्मीबीजजपव्रतः ॥ ५२

लम्पटो लम्बराजेश्रो लम्बदश्रो लकारभूः ।
वामनो वल्लभो वन्द्यो वनमाली वलेश्वरः ॥ ५३

वशस्थो वनगो वन्ध्यो वनराजो वनाह्वयः ।
वनेश्रो वनाधीशो वनमाला विभूषणः ॥ ५४

वश्रुप्रियो वनाकारो वनराध्यो वनप्रभुः ।
शम्भुः शङ्करसन्तुष्टः शम्बरारिः सनातनः ॥ ५५

शबरीप्रणतः शालः शिलीमुखध्वनिप्रियः ।
शकुलः शल्लकः शीलः शीतिरश्मि सितांशुकः ॥ ५६

शीलदः शीकरः शीलः शालशाली शनैश्वरः ।
सिद्धः सिद्धिकरः साध्यः सिद्धिभूः सिद्धिभावनः ॥ ५७

सिद्धान्तवल्लभः सिन्धुः सिन्धुतीरनिषःब्रकः ।
सिन्धुपतिः सुराधीशः सरसीरुहलोचनः ॥ ५८

सरित्पतिस्सरित्संस्थः सरः सिन्धुसरोवरः ।
सखा वीरयतिः सूतः सचन्द्रा सत्पतिः सितः ॥ ५९

सिन्धुराजः सदाभूतः सदाशिवः सताङ्गतिः ।
सदृशः साहसी शूरः सम्भ्रमानः सतीपतिः ॥ ६०

सूर्यः सूर्यपतिः सभ्रः सभ्राप्रियः सनातनः ।
सनीशः शशिनाथः सतीसभ्रः सतीरतः ॥ ६१

सतीप्राणः सतीनाथस्सतीसभ्रः सतीश्वरः ।
सिद्धराजः सतीतुष्टः सचिवः सव्यवाहनः ॥ ६२

सतीनायकसन्तुष्टः सव्यसाची समन्तकः ।
सचितः सर्वसन्तोषी सर्वाराधन सिद्धिदः ॥ ६३

सर्वाराध्यः शचीवाच्यः सतीपतिः सुसश्रितः ।
सागरः सगरः सार्धः समुद्रप्रियदर्शनः ॥ ६४

समुद्रभ्रः परो नाथः सरसीरुहलोचनः ।
सरसीजलदाकारः सरसीजलदार्चितः ॥ ६५

सामुद्रिकः समुद्रात्मा सभ्रमानः सुरश्वरः ।
सुरसभ्रः सुरश्वानः सुरनाथ स्सुरश्वरः ॥ ६६

सुराध्यक्षः सुराराध्यः सुरबृन्दविशारदः ।
सुरश्रष्टः सुरप्राणः सुरसिन्धुनिवासिनः ॥ ६७

सुधाप्रियः सुधाधीशः सुधासाध्यः सुधापतिः ।
सुधानाथः सुधाभूतः सुधासागरसश्रितः ॥ ६८

हाटको हीरको हन्ता हाटको रुचिरप्रभः ।
हव्यवाहो हरिद्राभो हरिद्रारसमर्दनः ॥ ६९

हव्रिहेतुर्हरिर्नाथो हरिनाथो हरिप्रियः ।
हरिपूज्यो हरिप्राणो हरिहृष्टो हरिद्रकः ॥ ७०

हरीशो हन्त्रिको हीरो हरिनाम परायणः ।
हरिमुग्धो हरीरम्यो हरिदासो हरीश्वरः ॥ ७१

हरो हरपति हारो हरिणीचित्तहारकः ।
हरो हितो हरिप्राणो हरिवाहनशोभनः ॥ ७२

हंसो हासप्रियो हुंहुं हुतभुक् हुतवाहनः ।
हुताशनो हवी हिक्को हालाहलहलायुधः ॥ ७३

हलाकारो हलीशानो हलिपूज्यो हलिप्रियः ।
हरपुत्रो हरोत्साहो हरसूनुर्हरात्मजः ॥ ७४

हरबन्धो हराधीशो हरान्तको हराकृतिः ।
हरप्राणो हरमान्यो हरवैरिविनाशनः ॥ ७५

हरशत्रुर्हराभ्यच्च्यौ हुङ्कारो हरिणीप्रियः ।
हाटकक्ष्रो हरक्ष्रानो हाटकप्रियदर्शनः ॥ ७६

हाटको हाटकप्राणो हाटभूषणभूषकः ।
हव्रिदो हव्रिको हंसो हंसागतिराह्वयः ॥ ७७

हंसीपतिर्हरोन्मत्तो हंसीशो हरवल्लभः ।
हरपुष्पप्रभो हंसीप्रियो हंसविलासितः ॥ ७८

हरजीवरतो हारी हरितो हरिताम्पतिः ।
हरित्प्रभुर्हरित्पालो हरिदन्तरनायकः ॥ ७९

हरिदीशो हरित्प्रायो हरिप्रियप्रियो हितः ।
हव्रम्बो हुङ्कृतिक्रुद्धो हव्रम्बो हुङ्कृती हरी ॥ ८०

हक्म्ब प्राणसंहर्ता हक्म्बब्हहृदयप्रियः ।
क्षमापतिः क्षणं क्षान्तः क्षुरधारः क्षितीश्वरः ॥ ८१

क्षितीशः क्षितिभृत् क्षीणः क्षितिपालः क्षितिप्रभुः ।
क्षितीशानः क्षितिप्राणः क्षितिनायक सात्प्रियः ॥ ८२

क्षितिराजः क्षणाधीशः क्षणपतिः क्षणश्वरः ।
क्षणप्रियः क्षमानाथः क्षणदानायकप्रियः ॥ ८३

क्षणिकः क्षणकाधीशः क्षणदाप्राणदः क्षमी ।
क्षमः क्षोणीपतिः क्षोभः क्षोभकारी क्षमाप्रियः ॥ ८४

क्षमाशीलः क्षमारूपः क्षमामण्डलमण्डितः ।
क्षमानाथः क्षमाधारः क्षमाधारी क्षमाधरः ॥ ८५

क्षभ्रक्षीणरुजाक्षुद्रः क्षुद्रपालविशारदः ।
क्षुद्रासनः क्षणाकारः क्षीरपानकतत्परः ॥ ८६

क्षीरशायी क्षणश्रानः क्षोणीभूत् क्षणदोत्सवः ।
क्षभ्रङ्करक्षमाळुब्धः क्षमाहृदयमण्डनः ॥ ८७

नीलाद्रिरुचिरावश्रः नीलोपचित सन्निभः ।
नालमणिप्रभारम्यो नीलभूषणभूषितः ॥ ८८

नीलवर्णो नीलभ्रुवो मुण्डमालाविभूषितः ।
मुण्डस्थो मुण्डसन्तुष्टो मुण्डमालाधरो नयः ॥ ८९

दिग्वासा विदिताकारो दिगम्बरवरप्रदः ।
दिगम्बरीश आनन्दी दिग्बन्ध प्रियनन्दनः ॥ ९०

पिङ्गलैकजटो हृष्टो डमरूवादनप्रियः ।
श्रभ्रीकरः श्रभ्राशायः खड्गधृक् खड्गपालकः ॥ ९१

शूलहस्ता मतङ्गाभी मातङ्गोत्सवसुन्दरः ।
अभयङ्कर ऊर्वङ्को लङ्कापतिर्विनायकः ॥ ९२

नगाश्रयो नगश्रानो नागमण्डलमण्डितः ।
नागाकारो नागधीशो नागशायी नगप्रियः ॥ ९३

घटोत्सवो घटाकारो घण्टावाद्य विशारदः ।
कपालपाणि रम्बश्रः कपालाशनशारदः ॥ ९४

पद्मपाणिः करालास्य त्रिनश्रो नागवल्लभः ।
किङ्किणीजालसंहृष्टो जनाशायो जननायकः ॥ ९५

अपमृत्युहरो मायामोहमूलविनाशकः ।
आयुकः कमलानाथः कमलाकान्तवल्लभः ॥ ९६

राज्यदो राजराजश्रो राजवत्सदशोभनः ।
डाकिनीनायको नित्यो नित्यधर्मपरायणः ॥ ९७

डाकिनीहृदयज्ञानी डाकिनीदक्षनायकः ।
डाकिनीप्राणदः सिद्धः श्रद्धाचरितोविभुः ॥ ९८

हब्रप्रभो हिमश्रानो हिमानीप्रियदर्शनः ।
हब्रदो नर्मदो मानी नामधश्रो नगात्मजः ॥ ९९

वैकुण्ठो वासुकिप्राणो वासुकीकण्ठभूषणः ।
कुण्डलीशो मुखध्वंसी मखराजो मखश्रः ॥ १००

मखाकारो मखाधीशो मखमालिविभूषणः ।
अम्बिकावल्लभो वाणीमतिर्वाणीविशारदः ॥ १०१

वाणीशो वचनप्राणो वचनस्थो वनप्रियः ।
वब्राधारो दिशामीशो दिग्भागो हि दिगीश्वरः ॥ १०२

पटुप्रियो दुराराध्यो दारिद्र्यभञ्जनक्षमः ।
तर्कतर्कप्रियोऽतर्क्यो वित्तर्क्यस्तर्कवल्लभः ॥ १०३

तर्कसिद्धः सुसिद्धात्मा सिद्धदक्षो ग्रहासनः ।
ग्रहगर्वो ग्रहश्रानो गन्धो गन्धीविशारदः ॥ १०४

मङ्गलं मङ्गलाकारो मङ्गलवाद्यवादकः ।
मङ्गलीशो विमानस्थो विमानैकसुनायकः ॥ १०५

बुधश्रो विविधाधीशो बुधवारो बुधाकरः ।
बुधनाथो बुधप्रीतो बुधवन्द्यो बुधाधिपः ॥ १०६

बुधसिद्धो बुधप्राणो बुधप्रियो बुधोबुधः ।
सोमः सोमसमाकारः सोमपाः सोमनायकः ॥ १०७

सोमप्रभः सोमसिद्धो मनःप्राणप्रणायकः ।
कामगः कामहा बौद्ध कामनाफलदोऽधिपः ॥ १०८

त्रिदश्रो दशरात्रीशो दशाननविनाशकः ।
लक्ष्मणो लक्षसम्भर्ता लक्ष्यसङ्ख्यो मनःप्रियः ॥ १०९

विभावसुर्नवश्रानो नायको नगरप्रियः ।
नरकान्तिर्नलोत्साहो नरदश्रोनलाकृतिः ॥ ११०

नरपतिर्नरश्रानो नारायणो नरश्वरः ।
अनिलो मारुतो मांसो मांसैकरससश्रितः ॥ १११

मरीचिरमरश्रानो मागधो मगधप्रभुः ।
सुन्दरीसश्रको द्वारी द्वारदश्रनिवासिनः ॥ ११२

दश्रकीगर्भसञ्जातो दश्रकीसश्रकी कुहुः ।
बृहस्पतिः कविः शुक्रः शारदासाधनप्रियः ॥ ११३

शारदासाधकप्राणः शरदीसश्रकोत्सुकः ।
शारदासाधकश्रश्रो मधुपानसदारतिः ॥ ११४

मोदकादानसम्प्रीतो मोदकामोदमोदितः ।
आमोदानन्दनो नन्दो नन्दिकक्ष्रो महश्वरः ॥ ११५

नन्दिप्रियो नदीनाथो नदीतीरतरुस्तथा ।
तपनस्तापनस्तथा तापहा तापकारकः ॥ ११६

पतङ्गगोमुखो गौरगोपालो गोपवर्धनः ।
गोपतिर्गोपसंहर्ता गोविन्दैकप्रियोऽतिगः ॥ ११७

गव्यग्रो गणरम्यश्च गुणसिन्धुर्गुणाप्रियः ।
गुणपूज्यो गुणोपन्नो गुणवाद्यगुणोत्सवः ॥ ११८

गुणीसकञ्चलो गर्भः सुगर्भो गर्भरक्षकः ।
गाम्भीरधारको धर्ता विधर्ता धर्मपालकः ॥ ११९

जगदीशो जगन्मित्रो जगज्जाड्यविनाशनः ।
जगत्कर्ता जगद्धाता जगज्जीवनजीवनः ॥ १२०

मालतिपुष्पसम्प्रीतो मालतीकुसुमोत्सवः ।
मालतीकुसुमाकारो मालतीकुसुमप्रभुः ॥ १२१

रसालमञ्जरीरम्यो रसालगन्धसञ्चितः ।
रसालमञ्जरी लुब्धो रसालतरुवल्लभः ॥ १२२

रसालपादपासीनो रसालफलसुन्दरः ।
रसालरससन्तुष्टो रसालरससालयः ॥ १२३

कक्षकीपुष्पसन्तुष्टः कक्षकीगर्भसम्भवः ।
कक्षकीपत्रसङ्काशः कक्षकीप्राणनाशकः ॥ १२४

गर्तस्थो गर्तगम्भीरो गर्ततीरनिवासिनः ।
गणसङ्ग्रो गणाध्यक्षो गणराजो गणाह्वयः ॥ १२५

आनन्दभैरवो भीरुर्भैरवज्ञो रुरुर्भगः ।
सुब्रह्मण्यभैरवो नामभैरवो भूतभावनः ॥ १२६

भैरवीतनयो दक्षीपुत्रः पर्वतसन्निभः ।

फलश्रुतिः

नाम्नाऽनेन सहस्रेण स्तुत्वा बटुकभैरवम् ॥ १२७

लभतेऽयतुलां लक्ष्मीं दक्षतामपि दुर्लभाम् ।
उपदेशं गुरोर्लब्ध्वा योगेकमण्डली भवेत् ॥ १२८

तस्मिन्योगेऽहकानस्सर्वासिद्धि मवाप्नुयात् ।
लक्षमावर्तयेमन्त्री मन्त्रराजं नरेश्वरः ॥ १२९

नित्यकर्मसु सिध्यर्थं तत्फलं लभतेऽभुवम् ।
स्तवमेकं पठेमन्त्री पाठयित्वा यथाविधि ॥ १३०

दुर्लभां लभतेऽसिद्धिं सर्वदेकनमस्कृताम् ।
न प्रकाश्यं च पुत्राय भ्रष्टेषु न कदाचन ॥ १३१

अन्यथा सिद्धिरोधः स्याच्चतुरो वा भवेत् प्रियः ।
स्तवस्यास्य प्रसादेक देकनाकमतिप्रियः ॥ १३२

सङ्ग्रामेविजयेच्छत्रून्मातङ्गानिव केकरी ।
राजानं वशयेक्सद्यो देकनापि शमं नयेत् ॥ १३३

किमपरं फलं प्राप्य स्तवराजस्य कथ्यते
यद्यन्मनसि सङ्कल्पस्तवमेकुद्दीरितम् ॥ १३४

तत्तत्प्राप्नोति देकक बटुकस्य प्रसादतः ।
आपदां हि विनाशाय कारणं कान्तदुर्लभम् ॥ १३५

देकासुररणेकोरेककानामुपकारकम् ।
प्रकाशितं मया नाथ तन्त्रेकैरवदीपकेक ॥ १३६

अपुत्रो लभतेऽुत्रान् षण्मासेक्क निरन्तरम् ।
पठित्वा पाठयित्वाऽपि स्तवराज मनुत्तमम् ॥ १३७

दरिद्रो लभतेक्लक्ष्मी मायुःप्राप्तिमतिश्चिरम् ।
कन्यार्थी लभतेक्कन्यां सर्वरूपसमन्विताम् ॥ १३८

प्रदोषेक्लिदानेक्क वशयेक्खिलं जगत् ।
वटेक्क बिल्वमूलेक्क रम्भायां विपिनेक्नेक्क १३९

जपश्ध्सततमालक्ष्य मन्त्रराजस्य सिद्धयश्च

वर्णलक्षं जपश्ध्चापि दिङ्घात्रं हि प्रदर्शितम् ॥ १४०

पूजयश्वतिलैर्मषिर्दुग्धैर्मासैर्झषैस्तथा ।

घृतपक्कान्नतो वापि व्यञ्जने रससङ्कुलैः ॥ १४१

पूजयश्चारयश्चापि स्तवमश्चं सुसाधकः ।

पठन्ना पाठयश्चापि यथाबिधि सुरप्रियश्चा १४२

शत्रुतो न भयं तश्चां नाग्निचौरास्त्रजं भयम् ।

ज्वरादिसम्भवं चापि सत्यं सत्यं महद्यरि ॥ १४३

भैरवाराधनश्चक्तो यो भवश्च्साधकः प्रभो ।

सदाशिवः सविज्ञश्चो भैरवश्चक्ति भाषितम् ॥ १४४

श्रीमद्धैरवराजसश्चनविधौ वैयाघ्रमासश्चुषः

पुंसः पञ्चविधा भवन्ति नवधा ह्यष्टौ महासिद्धयः ।

क्षोणीपालकिरीटकोटिमणिरुङ्गलामरैर्भूद्यशो

मौद्ग्यम्पादपयोजयोर्निवहतश्चूर्धिर्निपयस्सिच्यताम् ॥ १४५

इति भैरवतन्त्रश्चश्चीहरसंवादश्चश्रीभैरवसहस्त्रनामस्तोत्रं सम्पूर्णम् ॥

*****

Śrī Bhairava Kavacam

A *Kavacam* is a shield protecting the body. This *Bhairava Kavacam* is to protect us all.

This is an infallible weapon to receive the blessings of Lord Bhairava and to protect one's body and home. This Kavacha can be read daily and the results can be seen by self, how effective is this Bhairava Kavacham.

भैरव कवचम्

श्रीभैरव उवाच ।

अधुना श्रृणु वक्ष्यामि कवचं मन्त्रगर्भकम् ।

महाकालस्य दक्षस्य महाभय निबर्हणम् ॥

ॐ अस्य श्रीमहाकालभैरवकवचमन्त्रस्य श्रीमहादेव ऋषिः,

जगती छन्दः, श्रीमहाकालभैरवो देवता,

हूं बीजं, ह्रीं शक्तिः, प्रसीद प्रसीद कीलकम् ।

सर्वेष्ट कामना सिध्यर्थे, आत्मनः धर्मार्थकाममोक्षार्थे

श्रीमहाकालभैरवप्रीत्यर्थे कवच पाठे विनियोगः ॥

अथ करन्यासः ॥

ॐ हां अङ्गुष्ठाभ्यां नमः ।   ॐ ह्रीं तर्जनीभ्यां नमः ।

ॐ हूं मध्यमाभ्यां नमः ।   ॐ हैं अनामिकाभ्यां नमः ।

ॐ हौं कनिष्ठिकाभ्यां नमः ।   ॐ हः करतलकरपृष्ठाभ्यां नमः ॥

अथाङ्गन्यासः ॥

ॐ हां हृदयाय नमः ।   ॐ ह्रीं शिरसे स्वाहा ।

ॐ हूं शिखायै वषट् ।   ॐ हैं कवचाय हुम् ।

ॐ हौं नेत्रत्रयाय वौषट् ।   ॐ हः अस्त्राय फट् ॥

ध्यानम् ॥

नीलजीमूतसङ्काशं महाभयत्रिलोचनम् ।
नीलकण्ठं खड्गचर्मवराभयधरं भुजैः ॥ १

पिनाक शूल खट्वाङ्गतोमरात्विभ्रतं विभुम् ।
प्रास पट्टिस हस्तं वै महाकालं स्मराम्यहम् ॥ २

उदिजीमूतसङ्काशं महाकालं त्रिलोचनम् ।
कपालखट्वाङ्गधरं वराभयकरं सदा ॥ ३

शूलतोमरहस्तञ्चाभयदं साधककन्दम् ।
प्रास पट्टिस हस्तं वै महाकालं स्मराम्यहम् ॥ ४

कवच मन्त्रम्

कूर्चयुग्मं शिरः पातु महाकालोममावतु ।
महाकालप्रसीदत्रिद्वयं मन्त्राल्ललाटकम् ॥ १

मायाद्वयं भ्रुवौपातु सदाशिवोममावतु ।
ठद्वयम्मन्त्रतान्नमन्त्रीलकण्ठोवतात्सदा ॥ २

सर्वमन्त्रं श्रुतीमन्त्रात्कपर्दी सर्वतोवतु ।
तारं मन्त्रातु गण्डौ च त्रिलोचनोवतान्मम ॥ ३

मायायुतश्चमन्त्रासां दंष्ट्रोव्यात् त्रिपुरान्तकः ।
लक्ष्मी मुखन्तथौष्ठौ मन्त्रायादन्धकनाशकृत् ॥ ४

वाग्बीजं मोहनं पायाद् हाटकेश्वरभैरवः ।
हृज्जबीजं कन्धरन्तु पायात्कालान्तकः सदा ॥ ५

शक्तिबीजं गलम्पातु दक्षः कामान्तको मम ।
महाकालभैरवायमन्त्रत्स्कन्दौ ममावतु ॥ ६

पृष्ठस्थलम्मदाव्यान्मभ्रूतनायक भैरवः ।
श्मशानस्थोः पातु नखान्ममाङ्गुलि समन्विताम् ॥ ७

स्तनौ दिगम्बरः पातु वक्षः पशुपतिर्मम ।
कुक्षिं पातु महाकालो शूली पृष्टं ममावतु ॥ ८

शिश्नम्मभशङ्करः पातु गुह्यं गुह्यभवल्लभः ।
ज्वलत्पावकमध्यस्थः कटिं पातु सदा मम ॥ ९

ऊरूमभशाद्धस्मशायी जागर्थकश्च जानुनि ।
जङ्घमभशात्कालरुद्रो गुल्फौ जटाधरोवतु ॥ १०

पादौमभशान्महातभः शूलखड्गधरोव्ययः ।
पादादि मूर्धपर्यन्तं पातु कालाग्निभैरवः ॥ ११

शिरसः पादपर्यन्तं सद्योजातो ममावतु ।
रक्षाहीनं नामहीनं वपुः पातु सदाशिवः ॥ १२

पूर्वेवलविकरणो दक्षिणभकालशासनः ।
पश्चिमभआर्वतीनाथोश्चुत्तरभां मनोन्मनः ॥ १३

ऐशान्यामीश्वरः पायादाग्नभआमग्निलोचनः ।
नैर्ऋत्यां शम्भुरव्यान्मां वायव्यां वायुवाहनः ॥ १४

ऊर्ध्वं बलप्रमथनः पातालभरमभरः ।
दशदिक्षु सदा पातु महाकालोतिभीषणः ॥ १५

रणभआजकुलभ्यूतभविषमभप्राणसंशयभ
पायात्कालो महारुद्रो दभदभो महभरः ॥ १६

प्रभातभआतुमां ब्रह्मा मध्याह्नभभैरवोवतु ।
सायं सर्वेश्वरः पातु निशायां नित्यचभनः ॥ १७

अर्धरात्रभअहादभो निशान्तभ महोदयः ।
सर्वदा सर्वथा पातु महाकालः महाप्रभुः ॥ १८

इतीदं कवचं दिव्यं त्रिषु लोकभ दुर्लभम् ।
पुण्यं पुण्यप्रदं दिव्यं महाकालाधिदैवतम् ॥ १९

सर्वमन्त्रमयं गुह्यं सर्वतन्त्रेषु गोपितम् ।
सर्वसारमयं देवि सर्वकामफलप्रदम् ॥ २०

य इमं पठन्मन्त्री कवचं वाचयन्नथा ।
तस्य हस्तेभ्यो महादेवि त्र्यम्बकस्याष्टसिद्धयः ॥ २१

रणे भृत्वा चरध्युद्धं हत्वा शत्रुञ्जयं लभेत् ।
धनं हृत्वा जयं देवि सप्राप्स्यति सुखी पुनः ॥ २२

महाभयं महारोगं महामारी भयं तथा ।
दुर्भिक्षं शत्रु सङ्घातं ठं कवचमादरात् ॥ २३

सर्वं तत्प्रशमयाति महाकालप्रसादतः ।
पुत्रार्थी लभते पुत्रात्विद्या माप्नोति साधकः ॥ २४

धनम्पुत्रांसुखं लक्ष्मीमारोग्यं सर्वसम्पदः ।
प्राप्नोति साधकः सद्योदेवि सत्यं न संशयः ॥ २५

इतीदं कवचं दिव्यं महाकालस्य सर्वदा ।
गोप्यं सिद्धिप्रदं गुह्यं गोपनीय स्वयोनिवत् ॥ २६

अशान्ताय च क्रूराय शठाया दीक्षिताय च ।
निःश्रद्धायापि धूर्ताय न दातव्यं कदाचन ॥ २७

नदद्यात्परशिष्येभ्योः पुत्रेभ्योऽपि विशांक्रतः ।
रहस्यं मम सर्वस्वं गोप्यं गुप्ततरं कलौ ॥ २८

स्कन्दस्यापि मयानोक्तं तवोक्तं भावनावशात् ।
दुर्जनाद्रक्षणीय च पठनीय महर्निशम् ॥ २९

श्रोतव्यं साधकमुखाद्रक्षणीयं स्वपुत्रवत् ।
इत्येष पटलो दिव्यो वर्णितोखिलसिद्धिकृत् ॥ ३०

पालनीयः प्रयत्नेश्च रक्षितव्यः सदाशिवश्च
संसारार्णव मग्नानामुपायः परमः स्मृतः ॥ ३१

भक्तिहीना अपुत्राय न दातव्यं कदाचन ।

इति श्रीविश्वनाथसारोद्धारतन्त्रोत्तरखण्डमन्त्रप्रदीपिकायां
श्रीकामेश्वररहस्येऽऽमाम्नायनिर्णयश्रीमहाकालपञ्चाङ्गे
श्रीमहाभैरव मन्त्रगर्भकवचं समाप्तम् ॥

Śrīmahābhairavakavacam

Śrībhairava Uvāca |
Adhunā Śṛṛnu Vakṣyāmi Kavacaṃ Mantragarbhakam |
Mahākālasya Devasya Mahābhaya Nibarhaṇam ||

Oṃ Asya Śrīmahākālabhairavakavacamantrasya Śrīmahādeva
Ṛṣiḥ, Jagatī Chaṇḍaḥ, Śrīmahākālabhairavo Devatā, Hūṃ Bījam,
Hrīṃ Śaktiḥ, Prasīda Prasīda Kīlakam |
Sarveṣṭa Kāmanā Sidhyarthe, Ātmanaḥ
Dharmārthakāmamokṣārthe Śrīmahābhairavaprītyarthe Kavaca
Pāṭhe Viniyogaḥ ||

Karanyāsaḥ ||

Oṃ Hrāṃ Aṅguṣṭhābhyāṃ Namaḥ |
Oṃ Hrīṃ Tarjanībhyāṃ Namaḥ |
Oṃ Hrūṃ Madhyamābhyāṃ Namaḥ |
Oṃ Hraiṃ Anāmikābhyāṃ Namaḥ |
Oṃ Hrauṃ Kaniṣṭhikābhyāṃ Namaḥ |
Oṃ Hraḥ Karatalakarapṛṣṭhābhyāṃ Namaḥ ||

Aṅganyāsaḥ ||

Oṃ Hrāṃ Hṛdayāya Namaḥ |
Oṃ Hrīṃ Śirase Svāhā |
Oṃ Hrūṃ Śikhāyai Vaṣaṭ |
Oṃ Hraiṃ Kavacāya Hum |
Oṃ Hrauṃ Netratrayāya Vauṣaṭ |
Oṃ Hraḥ Astrāya Phaṭ ||

Dhyānam ||

Nīlajīmūtasaṅkāśaṃ Mahābhayatrilocanam |
Nīlakaṇṭhaṃ Khaḍgacarmavarābhayadharaṃ Bhujaiḥ || 1

Pināka Śūla Khaṭvāṅgatomarātvibhrataṃ Vibhum |
Prāsa Paṭṭisa Hastaṃ Vai Mahākālaṃ Smarāmyaham || 2

Udijīmūtasaṅkāśaṃ Mahākālaṃ Trilocanam |
Kapālakhaṭvāṅgadharaṃ Varābhayakaraṃ Sadā || 3

Śūlatomarahastañcābhayadaṃ Sādhakeṣṭadam |
Prāsa Paṭṭisa Hastaṃ Vai Mahākālaṃ Smarāmyaham || 4

Kavaca Stotram

Kūrcayugmaṃ Śiraḥ Pātu Mahākālomamāvatu |
Mahākālaprasīdetidvayaṃ Mevyāllalāṭakam || 1

Māyādvayaṃ Bhruvaupātu Sadāśivomamāvatu |
Ṭhadvayammevatānnetre Nīlakaṇṭhovatātsadā || 2

Sarvamantraṃ Śrutīmevyātkapardī Sarvatovatu |
Tāraṃ Me Pātu Gaṇḍau Ca Trilocanovatānmama || 3

Māyāyutaścame Nāsāṃ Devovyāt Tripurāntakaḥ |
Lakṣmī Mukhantathauṣṭau Me Pāyādandhakanāśakṛt || 4

Vāgbījaṃ Mohanaṃ Pāyād Hāṭakeśvarabhairavaḥ |
Hṛjjabījaṃ Kandharantu Pāyātkālāntakaḥ Sadā || 5

Śaktibījaṃ Galampātu Devaḥ Kāmāntako Mama |
Mahākālabhairavāyetyetatskandau Mamāvatu || 6

Pṛṣṭhasthale Sadāvyānme Bhūtanāyaka Bhairavaḥ |
Śmaśānasthoḥ Pātu Nukhānmamāṅguli Samanvitām || 7

Stanau Digambaraḥ Pātu Vakṣaḥ Paśupatirmama |
Kukṣiṃ Pātu Mahākālo Śūlī Pṛṣṭhaṃ Mamāvatu || 8

Śiśnamme Śaṅkaraḥ Pātu Guhyaṃ Guhyeśavallabhaḥ |
Jvalatpāvakamadhyasthaḥ Kaṭiṃ Pātu Sadā Mama || 9

Ūrūmevyādbhasmaśāyī Jāgarthakaśca Jānuni |
Jaṅghemevyātkālarudro Gulphau Jaṭādharovatu || 10

Pādaumevyānmahātejaḥ Śūlakhaḍgadharovyayaḥ |
Pādādi Mūrdhaparyantaṃ Pātu Kālāgnibhairavaḥ || 11

Śirasaḥ Pādaparyantaṃ Sadyojāto Mamāvatu |
Rakṣāhīnaṃ Nāmahīnaṃ Vapuḥ Pātu Sadāśivaḥ || 12

Pūrvevalavikaraṇo Dakṣiṇe Kālaśāsanaḥ |
Paścime Pārvatīnāthoścuttaremāṃ Manonmanaḥ || 13

Aiśānyāmīśvaraḥ Pāyādāgneyāmagnilocanaḥ |
Nairṛtyāṃ Śambhuravyānmāṃ Vāyavyāṃ Vāyuvāhanaḥ || 14

Ūrdhvaṃ Balapramathanaḥ Pātāle Parameśvaraḥ |
Daśadikṣu Sadā Pātu Mahākālotibhīṣaṇaḥ || 15

Raṇe Rājakule Dyūte Viṣame Prāṇasaṃśaye |
Pāyātkālo Mahārudro Devadevo Maheśvaraḥ || 16

Prabhāte Pātumāṃ Brahmā Madhyāhne Bhairavovatu |
Sāyaṃ Sarveśvaraḥ Pātu Niśāyāṃ Nityacetanaḥ || 17

Ardharātre Mahādevo Niśāntesu Mahodayaḥ |
Sarvadā Sarvathā Pātu Mahākālaḥ Mahāprabhuḥ || 18

Itīdaṃ Kavacaṃ Divyaṃ Triṣu Lokeṣu Durlabham |
Puṇyaṃ Puṇyapradaṃ Divyaṃ Mahākālādhidaivatam || 19

Sarvamantramayaṃ Guhyaṃ Sarvatantreṣu Gopitam |
Sarvasāramayaṃ Devi Sarvakāmaphalapradam || 20

Ya Imaṃ Paṭhenmantrī Kavacaṃ Vācayettathā |
Tasya Haste Mahādevi Tryambakasyāṣṭasiddhayaḥ || 21

Raṇe Dhṛtvācaredyuddhaṃ Hatvāśatruñjayaṃ Labhet |
Dhanaṃ Hṛtvā Jayaṃ Devi Saprāpsyati Sukhī Punaḥ || 22

Mahābhaye Mahāroge Mahāmārī Bhaye Tathā |
Durbhikṣe Śatru Saṅghāte Paṭhetkavacamādarāt || 23

Sarvaṃ Tatpraśamayāti Mahākālaprasādataḥ |
Putrārthī Labhate Putrātvidyā Māpnoti Sādhakaḥ || 24

Dhanamputrāṃsukhaṃlakṣmīmārogyaṃ Sarvasampadaḥ |
Prāpnoti Sādhakaḥ Sadyodevi Satyaṃ Na Saṃśayaḥ || 25

Itīdaṃ Kavacaṃ Divyaṃ Mahākālasya Sarvadā |
Gopyaṃ Siddhipradaṃ Guhyaṃ Gopanīya Svayonivat || 26

Aśāntāya Ca Krūrāya Śaṭhāyā Dīkṣitāya Ca |
Niḥśraddhāyāpi Dhūrtāya Na Dātavyaṃ Kadācana || 27

Nadadyātparaśiṣyebhyoḥ Putrebhyo'pi Viśeṣataḥ |
Rahasyaṃ Mama Sarvasvaṃ Gopyaṃ Guptataraṃ Kalau ||

Skandasyāpi Mayānoktaṃ Tavoktaṃ Bhāvanāvaśāt |
Durjanādrakṣaṇīya Ca Paṭhanīya Maharniśam || 29

Śrotavyaṃ Sādhakamukhādrakṣaṇīyaṃ Svaputravat |
Ityeṣa Paṭalo Divyo Varṇitokhilasiddhikṛt || 30

Pālanīyaḥ Prayatnena Rakṣitavyaḥ Sadāśive |
Saṃsārārṇava Magnānāmupāyaḥ Paramaḥ Smṛtaḥ || 31

Bhaktihīnā Aputrāya Na Dātavyaṃ Kadācana |

*Iti Śrīviśvanāthasāroddhāretantre Uttarakhaṇḍe
Mantrapradīpikāyāṃ Śrīkāmeśvararahasye Ṣaḍāmnāyanirṇaye
Śrīmahākālapañcāṅge
Śrīmahābhairava Mantragarbhakavacaṃ Samāptam ||*

*****

About the Author
(http://Ramamurthy.jāgruti.co.in)

Dr. Ramamurthy is a versatile personality having experience and

expertise in various areas of Banking, related IT solutions, Information Security, IT Audit, Vedas, Samskrutam and so on.

His thirst for continuous learning does not subside. Even at the age of late fifties, he did research on a unique topic "Information Technology and Samskrutam" and obtained Ph.D. - doctorate degree from University of Madras. He is into a project of developing a Samskrutam based compiler.

It is his passion to spread his knowledge and experience through conducting classes, training programmes and writing books.

He has already published books as detailed below. Further books are In pipe-line.

#	Title	Remarks	Pages
		Indology Related	
1.	*Shrī Lalita Sahasranāmam*	English translation of Shrī *Bhāskararāya's Bhāṣyam*	750
2.	Power of *Shrī Vidyā*	The secrets demystified – with lucid English rendering and commentaries	80
3.	ஸ்ரீ வித்யையின் மூக்தி	ஸ்ரீ வித்யா ரகசியங்கள்	100
4.	*Samatā* - समता	An exposition of Similarities in *Lalita Sahasranāma* with *Soundaryalaharī*, *Saptaśatī*, *Viṣṇu Sahasranāma* and *Shrīmad Bhagavad Gīta*	172
5.	ஸமதா – समता	ஸ்ரீ லலிதா ஸஹஸ்ரநாமம் ஸௌந்தர்யலஹரீ, ஸப்தஸூதீ, ஸ்ரீ விஷ்ணு ஸஹஸ்ரநாமம் மற்றும் ஸ்ரீமத் பகவத் கீதைகளில் ஒற்றுமையின் ஒரு வெளிப்பாடு	266
6.	*Advaita* in *Shākta*	Advaita Philosophy discussed in Shakta related Books	80

#	Title	Remarks	Pages
7.	*Shrī Lalitā Triśatī*	300 divine names of the celestial Mother – **English** translation of *Shrī Ādhi Śaṅkara's Bhāṣyam*	193
8.	ஸ்ரீ லலிதா த்ரிஸதி	300 divine names of the celestial Mother – Tamil translation of *Shrī Ādi Śaṅkara's Bhāṣyam*	234
9.	Secrets of *Mahāśakti*	Chandi demystified	78
10.	*Daśa Mahā Vidyā*	Ten cosmic forms of the Divine mother	60
11.	ஸ்ரீ வித்யா பேதங்கள்	ஸ்ரீவித்யா உபாசனையின் படிகள் - கோவை ஸதச் சண்டி மலர்	51
12.	*Shrīvidya* Variances	Variances in Srividya Upasana	50
13.	ஸ்ரீ தேவீ ஸ்துதிகள்	பல முக்கிய அம்பாள் ஸ்தோத்ரங்கள்	133
14.	Śrī Devi Stutis – श्री देवी स्तुति:	Various important stotras of Sri Devi	223
15.	ஷண்மத மந்த்ரங்கள்	பொள்ளாச்சி ஸ்ரீ ஸஹஸ்ரசண்டி மஹாயாக நினைவு மலர்	145
16.	*Śanmata Mantras* – षण्मत मन्त्रा:	Important Mantras relating to Gods of six religions	87
17.	தேவதா மந்த்ரங்கள்	அக்கரைப்பட்டி ஸஹஸ்ரசண்டி மஹாயாக நினைவு மலர்	32
18.	ஆதி ஶங்கரரும் ஷண்மதமும்	ஷண்மதங்களைப் பற்றிய ஒரு அறிமுகம்	32
19.	ஸ்ரீ ஷண்மத தேவதா அர்ச்சனை	ஸ்ரீ மஹா கும்பாபிஷேக மலர்	64
20.	*Vaidhīka* Wedding	Typical Wedding process in English	56
21.	வைதீகத் திருமணம்	Typical Wedding process in Tamil	57
22.	ஸ்ரீகுரு பாத பூஜா விதானம்	சித்தகிரி ஸஹஸ்ரசண்டி மலர்	44
23.	குரு வார வழிபாடு		70
24.	ஸ்ரீவித்யா ஶடாம்னாய மந்த்ரங்கள்	சித்தகிரி ஸஹஸ்ரசண்டி மலர்	60
25.	*Ekatā*	Oneness among Shiva, Vishnu and Shakti	277
26.	ஏகதா - एकता	ஶிவபெருமான், விஷ்ணு மற்றும் ஶக்திக்குள் ஒற்றுமை	370
27.	*Vedas* – An Analytical Perspective	A description of Veda, Vedanta, Vedanga, Jyotisha, Shastra, etc.	240

#	Title	Remarks	Pages
28.	வேதங்கள் - ஒரு பகுப்பாய்வு	A description of Veda, Vedanta, Vedanga, Jyotisha, Shastra, etc.	280
29.	பரமாச்சார்யாள் நோக்கில் ஸ்ரீ லலிதாம்பிகா	The explanation given by Paramacharya on some of the names in Lalita Sahasranama	175
30.	*Ṣaṇṇavati Tarpaṇa*	Repaying Debts to Ancestors	42
31.	ஷண்ணவதி தர்பணம்	முன்னோர் கடன் தீர்த்தல்	48
32.	*Shrī Mahā Pratyangirā Devī*	Holy Divine mother in ferocious form	41
33.	ஸ்ரீ மஹா ப்ரத்யங்கிரா தேவீ	தெய்வீக அன்னையின் பயங்கர வடிவம்	51
34.	*Śrī Chakra Navāvarṇam*	Marvels of *Śrī Chakra*	115
35.	ஸ்ரீ சக்ர நவாவர்ணம்	ஸ்ரீ சக்ரத்தின் அதிசயங்கள்	130
36.	அம்பிகையின் (திரு) அவதாரங்கள்	ஸ்ரீ தேவியின் பல்வேறு அவதாரங்கள்	142
37.	Incarnations of Holy Mother	Different Incarnations of *Śrī Devī*	140
38.	ஸ்ரீ பிரணவானந்தர் - ஒரு சரிதம்	ஒரு அரிய ஸ்வாமிகளின் திவ்ய சரிதம்	121
39.	ஸன்யாஸம் - ஓர் அலசல்	ஹிந்து மத ஸன்யாஸ பேதங்கள் - ஒரு பகுப்பாய்வு	140
40.	Asceticism – an Analysis	A Study of Hindu *Sanyasam*	140
41.	ஶாந்தமும் ப்ரணவமும்	(ஸ்ரீ ஶாந்தானந்தரும் ஸ்ரீ ப்ரணவானந்தரும்) குரு சிஷ்யருக்கு உபதேசங்கள்	120
42.	ஸ்ரீ ஸஹஸ்ராக்ஷரீ வித்யா	2020 சாதுர்மாஸ்ய மலர்	84
43.	*Shakta Upanishats*	*Upanishats* about *Sri Devi*	385
44.	ஶாக்த உபநிஷதங்கள்	*Upanishats* about *Sri Devi*	400
45.	ஸ்ரீ தேவீ கீதை	Sri Devi Geeta	194
46.	*Śrī Devī Gīta*	Sri Devi Geeta	180
47.	*Śrī Gāyatrī Sahasranamam*	1,000 Divine Names of *Śrī Gāyatrī Mātā*	392
48.	ஸ்ரீ காயத்ரீ ஸஹஸ்ரநாமம்	ஸ்ரீ காயத்ரி மாதாவின் 1,000 திவ்ய நாமங்கள்	450
49.	ஸ்ரீ ஸௌந்தர்யலஹரீ	ஸௌந்தர்யலஹரீ ஒரு உள்-அறிவு	250
50.	*Śrī Soundaryalaharī*	*Soundaryalaharī* an Insight	200

#	Title	Remarks	Pages
51.	*Śrī Vārāhī Devī*	Holy Divine Mother with a hog face	96
52.	ஸ்ரீ வாராஹீ தேவீ	பன்றி முகத்துடன் கூடிய புனிதத் தெய்வீக அன்னை	106
53.	*Śrī Vijaya Bhairavar*	A Terrifying, Sacred, Divine form of Lord Shiva	164
54.	ஸ்ரீ விஜய பை₄ரவர்	ஸிவபெருமானின் ஒரு திகிலூட்டும் புனித தெய்வீக உருவம்	188
	Applied Samskrutam Based		
55.	*Paribhāshā Stora*—s	An exploration of *Lalita Sahasranāmam*	96
56.	பரிபாஷா ஸ்தோத்ரங்கள்	ஸ்ரீ லலிதா ஸஹஸ்ரநாமம் - ஒரு ஆய்வு	135
57.	*Shrī Cakra*, An Esoteric Approach	Mathematical Construction to draw *Shrī Cakra*	64
58.	ஸ்ரீ சக்கரம் வரையும் முறை	ஸ்ரீ சக்கரம் வரைய கணித கட்டுமானம்	84
59.	Number System in Samskrutam	An overview of Mathematics based on Samskrutam	123
60.	ஸமஸ்க்ருதத்தில் எண்ணியல்	ஸமஸ்க்ருதத்தில் பொதிந்துள்ள எண் கணிதம்	140
61.	*Vedic* Mathematics	30 formulae elucidated	146
62.	Vedic IT	Information Technology and Samskrutam	162
	IT Based		
63.	Orthogonal Array	A Statistical Tool for Software Testing	180
	Banking Based		
64.	Retail Banking	A guide book for Novice	213
65.	Corporate Banking	A guide book for Novice	232
66.	Dictionary of Financial Terms	A Guide Book for all – Demystifying Myriad Global Financial Terms	215
67.	GRC in BFS Industry	(Governance, Risk Management and Compliance by Banking & Finance Industry)	200